nuevo cubano

COOKING

nuevo cubano

COOKING

★ ⌇ ★

SUE MULLIN

CHARTWELL
BOOKS, INC.

A QUINTET BOOK

Published by Chartwell Books
A Division of Book Sales Inc.
110 Enterprise Avenue
Secaucus, New Jersey 07094

This edition produced for sale
in the U.S.A., its territories
and dependencies only.

ISBN 1–55521–906–3

This book was designed and produced by
Quintet Publishing Limited
6 Blundell Street
London N7 9BH

Creative Director: Richard Dewing
Project Editor: Katie Preston
Editor: Beverly LeBlanc
Designer: Peter Laws
Photographer: Trevor Wood
Home Economist: Judith Kelsey

Typeset in Great Britain by
Central Southern Typesetters, Eastbourne
Manufactured in Hong Kong by
Regent Publishing Services Limited
Printed in Hong Kong by
Leefung-Asco Printers Limited

CONTENTS

Introduction

A joke periodically makes the rounds that Miami is the capital of Latin America, and that it is the only Latin metropolis where the phones work. In fact, phone service *is* good. Many phone lines in the area never faltered even during devastating Hurricane Andrew in 1992, a storm that ripped roofs off thousands of houses from South Miami on the mainland to the tip of the Keys, but graciously spared Miami's major tourist destination, scintillating Miami Beach.

But about that joke, as of the writing of this book, which went to press post-Andrew, Miami still was part of the United States, albeit a predominantly Latin city. It is a beautiful and bustling place where more than half the population speaks Spanish, where there are as many small cafés serving *Boliche* (a gourmet Cuban pot roast), *Ropa Vieja* (a shredded beef dish) and *Picadillo* (a complex ground beef concoction) as there are hamburger and hot dog stands. Miami is a city where the mayor is Cuban, a number of TV and radio stations are Cuban, and the place where the beans for the best espresso in the United States, known as *café cubano*, are roasted – a brew so rich and strong it's served in small plastic medicine cups and swallowed in one gulp like a shot of fiery bourbon.

Like *café cubano*, Miami is a bold and heady potion. Distinct from any other city in America, it

LEFT A symphony in pink – a perfectly matched Cadillac and Art Deco hotel on Miami's South Beach.

RIGHT A cool coffee bar on Calle Ocho is a perfect place to stop on a hot day.

is an adventure, a work in progress, a place that moves not to strident "broad shoulder" cadences of Chicago, nor the genteel rhythms of Boston, nor the cacophony of New York, but to an intoxicating, exhilarating Afro-Cuban beat.

Cubans fled their native island in droves during the years after Fidel Castro came to power in 1959, and they put their mark on every part of town. Glass skyscraper banks rose downtown, and Miami Beach, which had become a collection of cramped, run-down retirement apartments overlooking an oil-slicked ocean, also was transformed. South Beach now dazzles in the sun like a necklace of aquamarines and pink diamonds on the bodice of the Atlantic; its beaches are carpeted with bronzed bodies and the warm surf is dotted with bobbing swimmers. Ocean Drive boasts painstakingly restored art deco hotels painted in pastels and flashing

ABOVE Chess and card players in a shady area of Domino Park in Calle Ocho.

RIGHT Not even the skyscrapers in the background can spoil the beauty of this beach at Key Biscayne.

ABOVE This view of
Vizcaya shows the
strong Venetian
influence in the colors
and architecture, but the
palm trees would
certainly look out of
place in Italy.

RIGHT Two fishermen in
Naples, Florida, discuss
the day's catch.

RIGHT It is not surprising that Nuevo Cubano food uses a great variety of fish – with so much fresh fish from both the Gulf and the Atlantic.

neon signs like a less gaudy, tropical Las Vegas.

Each small gem of a hotel seems to have a sidewalk café and a post-modern design, air-conditioned, dining area inside. When European fashion photographers began flocking here a few years ago with their statuesque models in tow, Miami quickly gained trendy status. Restaurateurs were quick to notice the numbers of sophisticated people arriving and lured many top-notch chefs from across the country, Europe and Asia. Today, artists, fashion designers, actors, athletes, musicians, celebrities and tourists from Europe, Canada and South America vie for tables at the restaurants and cafés.

Not just at the beach, but throughout Miami, food – mouth-watering food – is never far away. It spills over sidewalks from open stalls of the *fruterias*, and it's sold from pushcarts and walk-up windows downtown and along Calle Ocho in Little Havana, as well as in Little Managua, Little Haiti, and large neighborhoods made up of Jamaicans, Dominicans and Puerto Ricans. Add to that mixed salad of cuisines the lace-curtain establishments of Coral Gables, Coconut Grove, Key Biscayne and North

Miami Beach, and you've got *muchas comidas* – many meals. Not even Hurricane Andrew stopped the flow of food for long. Street vendors were hawking fried cakes at busy intersections two days after Hurricane Andrew.

The exciting cuisine of Miami grew up along with its huge immigrant and exile communities. These transplants brought with them cravings for traditional island cuisine, replete with tropical fruits and tubers. Shortly after the Cubans arrived, for example, fruits such as mamey sapotes, the national fruit of Cuba, began to be grown commercially here in order to supply the local – and now worldwide – demand. The produce was so exotic to Americans that a New York food writer who took a cornucopia of it home with her a few years ago began to worry on the plane if she could get it through customs. Then she realized there would be no inspection since she had lever left the United States.

Traditional Cuban cuisine is itself an amalgam of Spanish, African and indigenous Indian ingredients and cooking techniques, and when you add to that the myriad influences on cooking in America,

LEFT South Beach, Miami, has been lovingly restored to its former Art Deco glory.

ABOVE A typical Southern-style house on Key West, Florida.

Nuevo Cubano can best be described in shorthand as New American with a conga beat. In traditional Miami-Cuban cookery, for example, much of the food is braised or fried, and roasts are stuffed with still other meats, such as chorizo and ham, and larded with bacon. In Nuevo Cubano, the emphasis is on lighter dishes, and fruit – which in Cuba is reserved mostly for snacks and milkshakes called *batidos* – is a major ingredient in many dishes and is widely used in creating colorful, edible garnishes.

Another hallmark of Nuevo Cubano cuisine is seafood. That's because Florida has the Atlantic on one side, the Gulf of Mexico on the other, and gigantic Lake Okeechobee and the Everglades in between. But I don't intend to send anyone on an alligator hunt (restricted to only one day per year in the Everglades) with this book or to teach anyone how to roast a whole pig over a spit as in traditional Cuban cooking. I hope to show you how you can take locally obtainable ingredients and bring a bit of Miami spice – in all its diversity and creativity, color and rhythm – to your table.

ABOUT THE INGREDIENTS

As you page through the book, you will notice that I have begun the chapters with Embellishments, a striking feature of Nuevo Cubano cuisine. I have laid the book out in this manner because so many of these salsas, relishes, dips, marinades, vinaigrettes, chutneys and butters jazz up the dishes in this book, but can enhance many other foods you are probably already making regularly. I have made some suggestions, but I'm sure you can come up with even more.

You'll notice Nuevo Cubano incorporates many tropical fruits, tubers and local seafood. With the possible exception of some of the seafood, the other ingredients are also used in many Caribbean, Latin American, Indian and Asian cuisines so do use this opportunity to explore any markets in your area specializing in fresh exotic produce. And don't fret if you can't find the fresh item. Great strides have been made in the variety and quality of canned and frozen fruits and vegetables. Just read the labels and try to ascertain that fruits, in particular, are not packed in heavy, sickening-sweet syrups.

I learned to love Nuevo Cubano cuisine before I found out how to cook it. I have spent the past few years in Miami as a restaurant critic, writing about a different spot each week. (It's a tough job but someone's got to do it.) Many of the dishes in this book are ones I first encountered in restaurants. Dishes such as Shrimp Hash Cakes, Malanga Pancakes with Caviar, Sherried Lobster Bisque and Citrus-Crusted Shrimp with Ginger Star Fruit and Rum, for example, were originally created by Miami's fine Nuevo Cubano chefs.

The unusual, tropical ingredients are introduced in a glossary at the end of this section. My hope is that by browsing through the book, referring to the glossary where necessary before embarking on, say, a huge dinner party featuring Nuevo Cubano cuisine, you will not be as ill-prepared for the experience as I was when I first came to Florida.

On a stroll one day in my new environment, I saw some sort of fruit on the sidewalk. There were many more of these strange looking, reddish-black objects on the ground in the adjacent yard so I figured since this one had fallen fortuitously on the public sidewalk, I could take it come, cut it open, compare it to some books I had purchased, and discern whether it was edible or not. Suddenly, an elderly woman came running from her house toward me. I feared she was going to upbraid me for stealing her fruit. Instead, she told me all about the object of my curiosity, a mango – way overripe as it turned out – and insisted on giving me three, beautiful, unbruised, reddish-orange ones straight from her refrigerator to take home, plus some tips and recipes.

Since that day years ago, I have happily explored many ingredients unheard of in my parents' generation – papayas, mamey sapotes, guava, cilantro, yuca, boniatos, malangas, conch, alligator and so much more. A new world of cuisine opened to me. I graduated from inspecting sidewalk fruit to collecting information and recipes in a more reputable manner: by trying out dishes using our regional cornucopia made by Miami's growing legion of excellent chefs and by replicating the outstanding creations, as closely as possible, in my own kitchen.

Now, I would like to pass the adventure of Nuevo Cubano cuisine on to you. I only hope I am half as gracious and knowledgeable as the sweet mango lady who set me on this course.

GLOSSARY

Here's a guide to southern Florida's and Cuba's rich and varied ingredients that lend so much to Nuevo Cubano cooking. Caribbean markets are a good source of many of these ingredients in other parts of the country.

SEAFOOD

Abalone Abalone is an earshaped shellfish with a pearly interior marketed canned or frozen by Mexico and Japan. Like conch, it is tough and needs a considerable amount of tenderizing by pounding, grinding, chopping, marinating and so forth. It is, however, a delicious fruit of the sea – as is conch. It's also native to California waters, but the catch is restricted and none of it is marketed commmercially on any broad scale.

Conch It's the meat inside the beautiful, big, spiral-shaped shells children put up to their ears in order to hear the ocean roar. In Florida, the word is pronounced "konk," as in the French word "conque" meaning shell – no one knows why. Secondly, the people of Key West are called conchs – ostensibly because they're strong and tough like conch meat, a label proudly worn.

Grouper More than 50 varieties of this predatory fish are found in the Florida coastal waters. The moist, firm flesh tastes similar to sea bass, which is a good substitute. Other acceptable substitutes include halibut, whitefish and snapper.

Marlin These game fish have firm, dense flesh with a rich flavor, that makes them ideal for grilling, broiling or frying. Shark and swordfish are good substitutes.

Pompano A king of the Atlantic coastal waters, considered by many to be Florida's finest fish, pompano's delicate white flesh commands high prices even in Miami. Sole is a more economical substitute. Pompano fillets are thin, but flavorful with a rich mild sea flavor. A noted French chef and restaurateur, Dominique D'Ermo, says that fillets (no more than ¾-inch thick) of red snapper, sea bass, flounder, or red salmon make good substitutes.

grouper

Red Snapper Abundantly available in the waters off Cuba as well as all around Florida, this white fish is shipped to markets all around the country. Similar to the grouper and sea bass, red snapper has a lean but firm flesh with a distinctive flavor. If not available, substitute any white, firm-fleshed fish, such as perch, turbot or sole.

VEGETABLES

Boniatos Boniatos are white-fleshed sweet potatoes. They have a texture similar to white potatoes and a more subtle, spicy sweetness than the vivid orange sweet potato Americans call (incorrectly) yams. It is believed that Columbus presented Queen Isabella with boniatos – not white spuds – and they quickly caught on in Europe for a time. You can cook them in most any style that you would use for white potatoes.

Guava Here's another so-called "exotic" fruit that is grown in many parts of the world, including Australia, South Africa and some parts of Southeast Asia, as well as in the American tropics. This walnut- to apple-sized fruit with lots of edible seeds embedded in the pulp tastes like strawberries to some, bananas to others, pineapple to still others and like nothing else in the world to the rest of us. It's ripe and sweet when it feels like a ripe pear.

Malanga Called yautia in Puerto Rico, this is a large, knobby, tuber that sometimes looks like a hairy caveman's club. Native to the Americas, it has an unusual nutty flavor that Cubans, Puerto Ricans and a growing number of Nuevo Cubano cuisine fanciers enjoy. If using white potatoes as a substitute for malanga, add about 1 tsp ground walnuts per ¼lb potato in order to approximate the unique flavor of malanga.

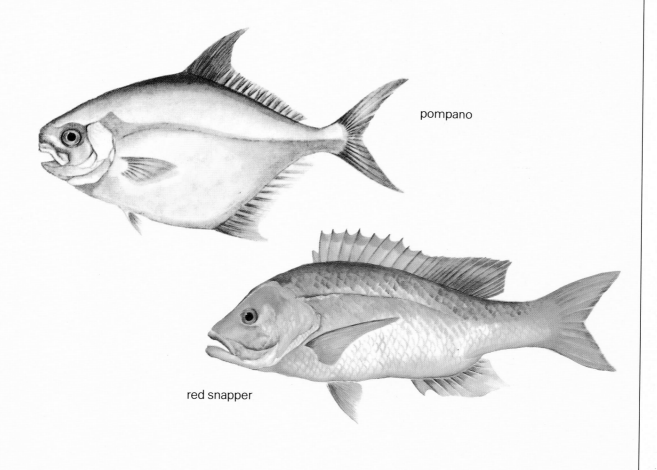

pompano

red snapper

Mamey Sapotes The sapote family is huge. But Cubans will immediately tell you that there is only one worth considering, and that the national fruit of the island has a rough, brownish skin, glorious, grainy, salmon-colored fruit inside, and a glistening black pit. The taste hints of peaches, cinnamon, and pumpkin.

Mango This fruit with juicy, sweet-tart, yellowish-orange flesh is to Miami and the Caribbean and, indeed, half the world what an apple is to those in apple-growing climates. Small Asian varieties are said to be the world's best. Most of the world's many types turn from green to variegated shades of yellow, orange and red when ripe. Select as you would other melons, lightly squeezing to make certain fruit is not hard and unripe. Some persons are allergic to mango juice and their skin will swell or blister upon touching it. Wear rubber gloves if you're concerned about this. There is no perfect substitute, but you could try a combination of the flavors in mango: peaches, pineapple and apricots.

Papaya Amusingly called *fruta bomba* by Cubans, the shrub that bears this fruit was being grown in the West Indies centuries before Columbus arrived. Cultivated pretty much year-round, this avocado-shaped, thin-skinned delight is usually green, hard and unripe when you see it at your neighborhood fruit market. So do the "ripe" thing: place it in a heavy, brown, grocery store bag, perforated with a few holes. After a few days at room temperature, the papaya will ripen to a rosy yellow hue and its flesh will be juicy and vivid orange and taste like a subtly perfumed combination of many other melons. Rather than a nut in the center, like an avocado, the papaya has a cavity filled with delicious black seeds that taste like watercress. Try the seeds in any salad or vinaigrette. As for the fruit itself, papaya – like mango – has an abrasive sap, so beware.

RIGHT chayote

BELOW plantain

ABOVE mango

ABOVE limes

ABOVE papaya

Passion Fruit This intensely flavored fruit is currently fancied by famous chefs the world over. Fortunately, a little passion fruit juice goes a long way because these fruits are quite expensive in many places in the world. The passion fruit's skin is sometimes a homely brown color, and the fruit inside is even more unusual looking – lots of edible seeds embedded in the pulp. But the passion fruit is noted for its symphony of tastes – citrus, pineapple and guava – and its perfumey aroma when it's perfectly ripe. Many fancy that it's named for secular passion, but, actually, the fruit takes its name from the tree's flowers and the symbolism of those is religious. The flowers have petals signifying Christ's wounds, crucifixion nails, crown of thorns and the Apostles – the Passion of Christ.

Plantains These are the big brothers of the banana family, but must be cooked. If a recipe calls for green plantains, look for green plantains, which are starchy and not sweet. If the dish calls for ripe plantains, look for ones that are turning from green to yellow-brown. If all you can find are green, place in a 300° oven until skin turns black and begins to split if you don't have days to allow them to ripen at room temperature.

Star Fruit Also called by its Indian name carambola, but the English name is so descriptive of this stunning little beauty. Its waxy yellow or white skin has five ribs and when it's sliced, you have an instant fruit sculpture of a five-pointed star! Furthermore, you can eat these "stars" as they are – no peeling necessary. White-skinned varieties generally taste sweet, like a combination of plums, apples, grapes and a hint of lemon. Yellow-skinned ones are usually a tad tart if they have very narrow ribs.

Yuca Called cassava by some, yuca is a homely, starchy tuber whose skin looks like bark. It is not the easiest thing to work with considering its tough skin and fibrous cord running through it, but no authentic Cuban pantry would be without it. Miami even has a Nuevo Cubano restaurant named for it. If you can't find yuca, you may substitute white potatoes.

RIGHT passion fruit

ABOVE star fruit

BELOW yuca

FLAVORINGS

Achiote Seeds From an American tropical tree called the Annatto which have been used for centuries as a yellow-orange food coloring. If you cannot find it, paprika will fill the bill just fine. Tastewise, achiote is so bland it is not worth worrying about.

Cilantro Also called Chinese parsley, Mexican parsley or fresh coriander, this herb has a broad, flat serrated leaf. It tastes very strong and distinctive, and for most tasters, it's love or hate at first bite. There really is no substitute, but most of the recipes in this book have a variety of seasonings that will hold up without it. Don't confuse cilantro with ground coriander, which is from the seed of the plant and has a different taste altogether.

Liquid smoke and smoked salt Both these products give a natural smoked or barbecued flavor to food. I believe we'll begin to see these products take off in popularity because while a lot of people like the taste of barbecued and/or smoked food, good outdoor equipment is expensive, cheap equipment is unwieldy and many people, such as those living in high-rise apartments, are not permitted to use barbecues and there are many others who live in cold climates where barbecuing is only feasible in the summer. Liquid smoke is dashed or brushed onto a variety of meats before, during, or after cooking. Smoked salt can be sprinkled over baked potatoes and used to season hamburgers, roasts, and steaks etc. You will find these products where barbecue equipment is sold or at specialist food stores.

Limes The Persian lime, which is about the size of a plum, is the most common. The Key lime, grown in the Florida Keys, is much smaller, and tarter.

Seville Orange A bitter fruit from the city in Spain for which it is named, this is used as a marinade. You can make a close substitute by combining 1 part unsweetened (naturally sweet) orange juice to ½ part lime juice and ½ part lemon juice.

ABOVE   mamey sapote

RIGHT oranges

COMPANY'S COMING

CHICKEN

Poached Chicken with Melon
Gingery Jasmine Rice
Warm Asparagus with Curry Butter
Chilled hearts of palm dressed with Curry-
Lime Vinaigrette
Catalan Creme Brulée

Broiled or Grilled Lime Chicken Breasts
with Sweet Pepper Chutney
Lime-Pepper Noodles
Chayote & Carrots
Rum Chiquitas

Lime-Baked Chicken Pieces served on bed
of Easy Black Bean Purée garnished with
snipped chives
Steamed white rice or Curried Almond
Rice
Grated Carrots with Ginger-Orange Mayo
Key Lime Pie

Mango Soup
Stovetop Creamy Chicken
Plantain-Apple Patties
White Chocolate Coconut Tart

FISH FARE & SEAFOOD

Shrimp-Chorizo Fajitas in Lettuce
Cilantro-Lime Grilled Tuna
Lime-Pepper Noodles
Passion Fruit Cup

Gazpacho Rioja
Nutty Roasted Red Snapper
Gingery Jasmine Rice
Catalan Creme Brulée

Black Bean Soup
Crisp Oven-Fried Flounder topped with
Garden Avocado Salsa
Mixed Green Salad with Curry-Lime
Vinaigrette
Key Lime Pie

Sherried Lobster Bisque
Citrus-Crusted Shrimp with Ginger
Starfruit and Rum
Churros & Espresso

Crab Cakes with Pepper-Lime Dip
Mia-Mex Starfruit & Black Bean Salsa
Corn on the Cob

Split-Pea Soup with Chorizo
Citrus-Crusted Shrimp with Ginger
Starfruit and Rum
Tostones con Brie
Pink Coleslaw

Sherried Lobster Bisque
Salmon in Romaine Fajitas
Skewered Grilled Onion Wedges and
Tomato Halves with Pepper-Lime Dip
Mango Sorbet

Malanga Pancakes with Caviar
Juicy Swordfish with Pineapple-Coconut
Relish
Gingery Jasmine Rice
Cantaloupe Sorbet

Lobster-Mango Cocktail
Pecan-Encrusted Flounder in Tango-
Mango Butter Sauce
So-Sweet Sweet Potatoes and Carrots
Pasta with Beans, Cuban-style
Café con Leche Custard

Shrimp Hash Cakes atop Plantain-Apple
Patties in Mango Mustard
Corn Cubana
Oven-Baked Tropical Chips
No-Cook Rum Chiquitas

White Bean & Yuca Vichyssoise
Crab Cakes
Chayote and Carrots
Curried Almond Rice
Café con Leche Custard

Assortment of Crackers with Smoked
Grouper Spread
Seafood Linguine
Pink Coleslaw
White Chocolate Coconut Tart

BEYOND MEAT & POTATOES

Pop Eye's Pork Tenderloin with Pineapple-
Coconut Relish
Plantain-Apple Patties
Pasta Fagioli Cubano
Key Lime Pie

Fruited Crab Salad
Purple Peppered Penne with Chorizo
Chayote and Carrots
White Chocolate Coconut Tart

White Bean & Yuca Vichyssoise
Grilled Isla Bonita Pork with Pineapple
Salsa
Plantain-Apple Patties
Churros and Espresso

Black Bean Soup
Elegante Picadillo over Herbed Rice Cakes
Mango Sorbet

Sherried Lobster Bisque
Ropa Vieja in Warmed Flour Tortillas,
topped with Sofrito, and garnished with
Pimientos
Corn Cubana
No-Cook Rum Chiquitas

Boliche
Curried Almond Rice
Lima Beans in Warm Citrus-Mushroom
Salsa
Catalan Creme Brulée

Embellishments

salsas, relishes, & dips
marinades & vinaigrettes
chutneys
butter logs

Much of the color, texture and style in South Florida's cuisine is in the embellishment of a dish – before, during, or after cooking it. This is especially true of marinades. Because most meats and poultry have less fat content these days, the acid in a marinade serves to tenderize and keep a lean cut, such as a chicken breast, from turning out tough and dry. Fish and seafood also benefit greatly from the moisture and infusion of flavor. And when serving a plain fillet of fish, nothing looks prettier than a dollop of, say, pineapple chutney. It doesn't stop at appearances, though. The chutney brings out the fish's flavor, as well.

These festive marinades and condiments are easy to make – only a few of them require any cooking at all – and give many plain dishes a gourmet touch. If you and your family and friends become particularly fond of some of these, consider serving the thicker, fruitier ones on breakfast rolls and waffles, or as salads. These recipes should easily yield four small salads. If a portion is left over from a meal, simply pop in the refrigerator for another use. Most will keep two to three weeks.

The butter logs are also versatile. In addition to basting with them and topping hot vegetables and entrees with them, you can sauté with them and slather them on warm breads, rolls, and all sorts of crackers. The chutneys are a special treat when spread atop crackers spread with cream cheese.

You'll want to keep your favorite butters on hand, too, and it's easy to do because they keep well. Refrigerate in a covered jar where they'll keep for about two weeks. Or cut off as much as you need and freeze the rest. A log will keep up to three months in the freezer. Next time you want to serve an elegant meal on short order, cut a few more pats off the log, allow the butter to reach room temperature, and you're all set.

LEFT A coffee stall on Calle Ocho, Miami.

SALSAS, RELISHES & DIPS

MIA-MEX STAR FRUIT AND BLACK BEAN SALSA

Complements broiled or grilled fish and poultry dishes, especially Lime-Baked Chicken Pieces (page 94).

- one 8-oz can black beans, drained
- ¾ cup corn kernels, fresh, frozen or canned and drained
- 8 oz ripe tomatoes, chopped
- 4 scallions, trimmed and chopped
- ½ green bell pepper, seeded and finely diced
- ½ sweet red pepper, seeded and finely diced
- 2 tbsp olive oil
- ½ cup red wine vinegar
- hot-pepper sauce to taste
- Worcestershire sauce to taste
- ground cumin to taste
- salt and fresh-ground black pepper to taste
- 1 star fruit, ½ sliced crosswise in thin sections, ½ diced

Mix the beans with the corn, tomatoes, onions, peppers, olive oil and vinegar and season to taste with the hot-pepper sauce, Worcestershire sauce, cumin and salt and pepper. Stir diced star fruit slices into the mixture and place the others across the top. Cover and refrigerate at least 3 hours to allow flavors to blend, then serve chilled.

PAPAYA-MANGO SALSA

Complements swordfish, trout, blue fish, catfish, grilled or broiled beef, grilled shrimp, sliced cold roast beef and Nutty Roasted Red Snapper (page 91).

- ½ papaya, peeled, seeded and cut into bite-size cubes
- ½ mango, peeled and cut into bite-size cubes
- 1 fresh jalapeño pepper, seeded and minced
- 1 green onion, minced
- 1 tbsp sugar
- 1 tbsp chopped fresh cilantro
- 1 tbsp finely chopped sweet red pepper
- papaya seeds to taste (optional)

In a medium bowl, combine all ingredients, cover and refrigerate. Serve chilled.

GARDEN AVOCADO SALSA

Complements Broiled or Grilled Lime Chicken Breasts (page 96), or can replace a salad on any menu. Great dip for taco chips, too.

- 1 cucumber, peeled, seeded and chopped
- 1 sweet red pepper, seeded and chopped
- 1 cup peeled, seeded and chopped fresh tomatoes
- 1 cup peeled and cubed avocado
- ½ cup diced red onion
- 1 tbsp white wine vinegar
- 1 tsp granulated sugar
- ½ tsp ground cumin
- ¼ tsp salt
- papaya seeds to taste (optional)

In small bowl, combine all ingredients, cover and refrigerate. Serve chilled.

PAPAYA-MANGO SALSA

PINEAPPLE SALSA

STOPLIGHT SALSA

Complements any fish or seafood dish, especially Cilantro-Lime Grilled Tuna (page 84).

- fresh-squeezed juice of 1 lime
- 2 ripe avocados, peeled and cut into bite-size chunks
- 2 pints cherry tomatoes, stemmed and quartered
- 5 cups frozen or canned corn kernels, drained
- 1 tbsp olive oil
- 2 tbsp chopped fresh cilantro
- ¼ tsp minced garlic
- salt and fresh-ground black pepper to taste
- hot-pepper sauce to taste (optional)
- papaya seeds to taste (optional)

Squeeze lime juice over avocados. Toss tomatoes and corn with olive oil. Combine avocados with tomato-corn mixture and season with cilantro, garlic, salt, pepper and hot sauce. Sprinkle a few papaya seeds on top, if you like.

PINEAPPLE SALSA

Complements ham and pork dishes, such as Grilled Isla Bonita Pork (page 101).

- 2 cups peeled and cored fresh ripe pineapple, or canned crushed pineapple in own juice
- 3 tbsp chopped fresh cilantro
- 2 tsp fresh-squeezed lime juice
- ⅛ tsp ground cumin
- ⅛ tsp fresh-ground white pepper

In a medium bowl, combine all ingredients, cover and refrigerate. Serve chilled.

WARM CITRUS-MUSHROOM SALSA

Complements Nutty Roasted Red Snapper (page 91), grilled or broiled fish, seafood or poultry dishes, roast beef dinners, warm green vegetables, such as broccoli, brussel sprouts, green beans and lima beans.

- 1 tbsp olive oil
- 2 shallots, or white part of 4 scallions, peeled and minced
- 8 oz (5½ cups) fresh mushrooms, trimmed and thinly sliced
- ½ cup orange juice
- ½ cup bottled clam juice
- salt and fresh-ground black pepper to taste
- ¼ cup parsley or cilantro leaves, minced

In a large skillet over medium heat warm oil. Add shallots and cook 1 minute. Add mushrooms and cook a few seconds to soften slightly. Add orange juice and clam juice and bring to a boil. Simmer 5–7 minutes, until mushrooms are tender. Uncover and boil over high heat until liquid is slightly thickened, about 5 minutes. Season with salt and pepper and stir in parsley or cilantro.

DELICATO MANGO SALSA

Complements baked scallops and *Ensalada de Moros y Cristianos* (page 67).

- 2 mangoes, peeled and diced
- ½ cup dry white wine
- 3 tbsp light olive oil
- salt and fresh-ground white pepper to taste

Simmer mango slowly in wine until soft. Purée in blender or food processor, return to heat and whisk in olive oil. Season with salt and pepper. Set aside, keep warm until served.

STAR FRUIT SALSA

Complements broiled or grilled fish, chicken or pork. Makes a jazzy stuffing for avocado halves.

- 5–6 star fruit, seeded and cut into large chunks
- 1 green bell pepper, seeded and diced
- 2 sweet red peppers, seeded and diced
- 1 onion, chopped
- 1 clove garlic, minced
- fresh-squeezed juice of 2 Key or Persian limes
- dash hot-pepper sauce
- salt to taste

In a small bowl, combine all ingredients, cover and refrigerate. Serve chilled.

LEFT Calle Ocho – a principal tourist destination in Miami.

PINEAPPLE-COCONUT RELISH

EASY BLACK BEAN PURÉE

Complements chicken and fish entrées.

- 1 cup canned black beans (not drained)
- 1 tbsp balsamic vinegar, or lime juice, or fresh Seville orange juice
- salt and fresh-ground black pepper to taste
- 2 tbsp chopped red onion
- 1 sweet red pepper, seeded and diced

Mix beans and vinegar, lime juice, or Seville orange juice together. Purée in a blender or food processor. Add salt and pepper to taste. Warm.

Spoon on a plate and place chicken or fish over the sauce. Sprinkle the top with the onion and red bell pepper.

PINEAPPLE-COCONUT RELISH

Complements Sautéed Snapper (page 88) or any fish, chicken or duck dish.

- ⅔ cup diced ripe pineapple
- ½ cup seeded and diced yellow bell pepper
- ½ cup diced red onion
- ½ cup diced hot pepper
- ½ cup unsweetened shredded dry coconut
- 1 tbsp sherry vinegar

Combine all ingredients in bowl. Cover and let stand at room temperature for at least 10–15 minutes until ready to serve.

SIMPLE GARLICKY AIOLI

Complements boiled, baked, poached or sautéed fish, green beans, Yuca Fries (page 110), Conch Fritters (page 64), Codfish Fritters (page 60) and any dish that can use a shot of garlic.

- 2 cloves garlic, crushed
- ½ cup mayonnaise

Stir together and serve chilled.

GINGER-ORANGE MAYO

Complements Chicken Mango Salad (page 69), cold or warm cooked carrots or cauliflower, a fillet of fish or baked sweet potato. Also toss this with salad greens or use as dip for Plantain Rounds with Brie (page 112).

- 1½ cups mayonnaise
- 6 tbsp orange juice
- 4 tbsp fresh-squeezed lime juice
- 3 tsp grated orange zest
- 4 tsp grated fresh ginger root
- fresh-ground white pepper to season

Combine all ingredients, cover and refrigerate. Serve chilled.

GINGER-ORANGE MAYO

PEPPER-LIME DIP

Complements artichokes, lobster, scallops, crab claws, Crab Cakes (page 80), stone crabs, Alaskan King Crab legs and Monkfish in Banana Leaves (page 92).

- ½ tsp salt
- 1 clove garlic, minced
- 1 small hot pepper, seeded and minced
- ⅓ cup fresh-squeezed lime juice
- ⅓ cup minced onion
- 6 tbsp cold water
- 1–2 tbsp minced fresh cilantro (optional)

Mash salt with garlic and hot pepper to form a paste. Stir in lime juice, onion, water and cilantro, if desired. Let stand 1 hour before serving.

BELOW The pastel shades of the Art Deco buildings on South Beach complement the natural surroundings perfectly.

SWEET AND SASSY MANGOLADE DIP

Complements chicken or Codfish Fritters (page 60), fish fillets coated with nuts, grilled chicken, Shrimp Hash Cakes (page 90) and Sautéed Snapper (page 88).

- ¾ cup prepared mango chutney, coarsely chopped
- 1 cup orange marmalade
- ½ cup grainy mustard
- 1 tbsp bottled horseradish or to taste

Combine all ingredients, cover and refrigerate. Serve chilled.

VODKA DIP

Complements Alaskan King Crab legs, stone crabs,
Conch Fritters (page 64), Crab Cakes (page 80)
and Malanga Pancakes (page 63).

- 1 cup mayonnaise
- 1 tbsp tomato paste
- ¼ cup vodka
- ¼ cup chopped scallions
- ¼ cup chopped fresh parsley

- 2 tbsp lemon juice
- 1 tsp ground cumin
- ⅛ tsp hot-pepper sauce

In a small bowl, whisk mayonnaise with tomato paste, then whisk in remaining ingredients. Cover and refrigerate at least 3 hours or overnight.

LIME MUSTARD

This delicious mustard complements Conch Fritters (page 64), Codfish Fritters (page 60), and any breaded fish dish.

- 2 cups mayonnaise
- ¼ cup Dijon mustard
- ¼ cup fresh-squeezed Key, Persian or regular lime juice
- 1½ tsp grated lime zest
- 2 tbsp hot-pepper sauce
- 2 tbsp Worcestershire sauce
- salt and fresh-ground black pepper to taste
- cayenne pepper to taste
- papaya seeds to taste (optional)

In a small bowl, combine all ingredients, cover and refrigerate. Serve chilled.

MANGO MUSTARD

Complements Conch Fritters (page 64) and fried fish or seafood, especially breaded ones, and Sandwiches Nuevo Cubano (page 59).

- ¾ cup olive oil
- 1 cup Dijon mustard
- 1 cup dry white wine
- ¼ cup puréed fresh, frozen or drained unsweetened canned mango
- 1 tsp garlic salt
- 2 tbsp soy sauce
- papaya seeds to taste (optional)

Whisk oil into mustard and wine. Stir in mango purée, garlic salt, soy sauce and papaya seeds, if desired. Cover and refrigerate. Serve chilled.

LEFT
LIME MUSTARD

MARINADES & VINAIGRETTES
SOFRITO

Sofrito comes from the Spanish verb meaning "to sauté." This thick tomato-pepper salsa is also a staple in Cuban kitchens.

Complements chicken and rice dishes, Basque-style cod dishes and omelets, or use it to spread on tortillas for fajitas or Ropa Vieja (page 102).

- 2 onions, finely chopped
- 1 large green bell pepper, seeded and diced
- 5 cloves garlic, mashed
- ½ cup olive oil
- one 4-oz jar diced pimentos, drained
- one 8-oz can tomato sauce
- 1 tsp dried oregano
- 1 tbsp red wine vinegar

In a large skillet over low heat, sauté onions, green pepper and garlic in the olive oil until tender and lightly browned, for about 15 minutes. Add pimentos and cook 5 more minutes over low heat. Add tomato sauce, oregano and vinegar and cook 10 more minutes. Let cool, then store in tightly closed jar in refrigerator up to 2 weeks.

CURRY-LIME VINAIGRETTE

Complements salmon, chicken, artichokes, mushrooms and asparagus. Splash over the filling for Salmon Fajitas (page 92) and Lobster-Mango Chutney (page 53).

- 1½ tsp grated finely lime zest
- ¼ cup fresh-squeezed lime juice
- 4 tbsp curry powder
- ½ cup safflower oil
- salt and fresh-ground white pepper to taste
- papaya seeds to taste (optional)

In a medium bowl, combine zest and lime juice. Whisk in curry powder, safflower oil and desired seasoning. Stir well and serve at room temperature.

No-Cook Mojito

The traditional Cuban table is never without this versatile seasoning sauce. It is to Cubans what ketchup is to Americans, except far more macho and potent.

Use as marinade for chicken and pork dishes.

Complements meats, fish and seafoods as they're being broiled or grilled. Splash over Oven-Baked Tropical Chips (page 113) and Yuca Fries (page 110).

- 4 cups fresh-squeezed Seville orange juice (about 20 oranges)
- fresh-squeezed juice of 4 limes
- 2 cups olive oil
- 12 cloves garlic, crushed
- 8 tbsp finely chopped onion
- 4 tbsp dry sherry
- 4 tsp salt
- 4 tsp dried oregano
- 2 tsp ground cumin
- ¼ cup minced fresh ginger root

Stir together Seville orange and lime juices. Blend in oil and then garlic, onion, sherry, salt, oregano, cumin and ginger root. Place in a bottle or jar with a tight-fitting lid and refrigerate at least 1 day before using. Keeps about 2 weeks in refrigerator.

RIGHT Española Way near South Beach, Miami.

TOMATO-GINGER CHUTNEY

Complements Skirt Steak Fajitas (page 62), beef
and pork roasts, too.

- 1 head of garlic, minced
- 4 oz fresh ginger root, peeled and minced
- 1 cup rice wine or cider vinegar
- ¼ cup sugar

- 1 tsp salt
- 1 tsp cayenne pepper
- 1½ lb plum tomatoes, peeled, seeded and chopped

In a heavy saucepan, stir together all ingredients. Simmer over a low to moderate heat, stirring occasionally, until liquid is reduced by half. Cool to room temperature before serving.

SWEET PEPPER CHUTNEY

Complements Plantain Rounds with Brie (page 112), meats, fish and broiled poultry. Use as a topping for pizzas and a stuffing for turnovers.

- 2 tbsp olive oil
- 1 purple onion, chopped
- 3 cloves garlic, crushed
- 3 tbsp wine vinegar
- 2 tbsp brown sugar
- 1 tbsp corn syrup
- 1 tbsp mustard seeds
- 1 tbsp ground cloves

- ½ tsp ground mace
- ½ tsp ground allspice
- 1 tsp ground cinnamon
- 5 sweet red peppers, seeded and cut in strips
- salt and fresh-ground pepper to taste

In a skillet, heat oil and lightly fry onion and garlic until tender. Add vinegar, sugar, syrup, mustard seeds and spices. Mix well, add red peppers and cook 2 minutes. Season to taste. Serve warm or at room temperature.

SMOOTH "N" SASSY BUTTER LOGS

General Instructions

Use lightly salted or unsalted butter, according to your preference. You may even use margarine, but the taste will probably not be as rich. When butter has reached room temperature, beat all ingredients in a small bowl. Transfer mixture in the shape of a 12-inch log onto a piece of freezer paper or plastic wrap and roll up, twisting the ends of the paper like a party popper to seal. Refrigerate until firm or freeze. Each yields about a dozen 1 tsp pats. Only this first butter log requires cooking. On the others, simply follow the directions in this paragraph.

CURRY BUTTER LOG

Complements rice dishes, grilled or broiled shrimp or chicken, plain hot vegetables, such as corn, carrots, green beans, spinach and asparagus, and broiled tomatoes (add a sprinkling of cracker crumbs over melted butter).

- ½ cup minced onion
- 1 cup (2 sticks) butter, softened and divided in half
- 2 tbsp curry powder
- 4 tbsp prepared chutney, minced
- ½ tsp fresh-ground white pepper

In a small skillet over moderately low heat, cook onion in half of the butter, stirring until softened. Stir in curry powder, chutney and white pepper. Let mixture cool.

In a bowl, cream together remaining butter and the curry mixture.

SAFFRON-ORANGE BUTTER LOG

Use as dip for lobster, and drizzle over scallops, steamed or grilled shrimp, steamed white rice and asparagus.

- 1 cup (2 sticks) butter, softened
- finely grated zest of 2 oranges
- 1 tsp finely minced saffron

RIGHT
CURRY BUTTER LOG

44

LIME-CHIVE BUTTER LOG

Use to sauté Stovetop Creamy Chicken (page 97) veal or pork chops and drizzle over seafood or fish.

- 1 cup (2 sticks) butter, softened
- ½ cup finely snipped fresh chives
- 2 tbsp frozen lime juice concentrate, thawed
- 1 tbsp chopped fresh thyme or ½ tsp ground thyme

SMOKED PINEAPPLE BUTTER LOG

Use as dip for grilled lobster, shrimp or scallops.

- 1 cup (2 sticks) butter, softened
- ½ cup canned pineapple,
- drained and finely chopped
- 1 tsp liquid smoke

RIGHT
SMOKED PINEAPPLE BUTTER LOG

TANGO MANGO BUTTER LOG

If you can't find mangoes, substitute 4 oz peach and 4 oz pineapple puréed together. Use to sauté Pecan-Encrusted Flounder (page 84) or Sautéed Snapper (page 88).

- 1 cup (2 sticks) butter, softened
- 8 oz fresh or canned mango, peeled or drained and puréed
- 2 tsp freshly-squeezed lime juice
- 2 tbsp finely chopped fresh mint
- 1 tsp grated nutmeg

LEFT
TANGO MANGO BUTTER LOG

BELOW An international foodcourt near the central arts complex attracts workers from offices all over Miami.

CHIVE-MUSTARD BUTTER LOG

Drizzle on fish, chicken, veal or steamed vegetables. Spread on sandwiches and use as a topping for baked potatoes.

- 1 cup (2 sticks) butter, softened
- 6 tbsp snipped fresh chives
- 4 tbsp Dijon-style mustard
- 2 tsp lemon juice
- ½ tsp fresh-ground white pepper
- pinch salt

LIME-TOMATO BUTTER LOG

Use as dip for artichokes.

- 1 cup (2 sticks) butter, softened
- ½ cup dry-packed sun-dried red tomatoes, minced
- 2 tbsp frozen lime juice concentrate, thawed
- 1 tbsp minced fresh basil

CITRUS-PARSLEY BUTTER LOG

Spread on French bread and then top with a cucumber slice and a strip of smoked salmon.

- 1 cup (2 sticks) butter, softened
- 2 tsp grated orange zest
- 6 tbsp fresh-squeezed orange juice
- 2 tsp grated lemon zest
- 2 tsp fresh-squeezed lemon juice
- 2 tsp grated Persian lime zest
- 4 tsp fresh-squeezed Persian lime juice
- 6 tbsp minced fresh parsley
- salt and fresh-ground black pepper to taste

AVOCADO BUTTER LOG

Slather this on warm flour tortillas for a rich and nutty-tasting treat. Top with some drained water chestnut slices, jicama, bean sprouts, or cucumbers for a crunchy munchie.

- 1 cup (2 sticks) butter, softened
- ½ 8-oz avocado, peeled, pitted and cut into small chunks
- 2 tbsp fresh-squeezed Persian lime juice
- 2 tbsp chopped fresh parsley
- 2 tsp Worcestershire sauce
- ½ tsp minced garlic
- 2 drops hot-pepper sauce

ISLAND CITRUS BUTTER LOG

Use to sauté Pecan-Encrusted Flounder (page 84), and drizzle on fresh-cooked green beans, cauliflower, broccoli or asparagus.

- 1 cup (2 sticks) butter, softened
- 3 tbsp frozen orange, lime or lemon juice concentrate, thawed
- 2 tbsp grated lime zest
- pinch grated nutmeg

LEFT A street café on South Beach in the early evening, where the patrons can sit and admire the Cadillac parked out front while sipping their coffee.

RIGHT
ISLAND CITRUS BUTTER LOG

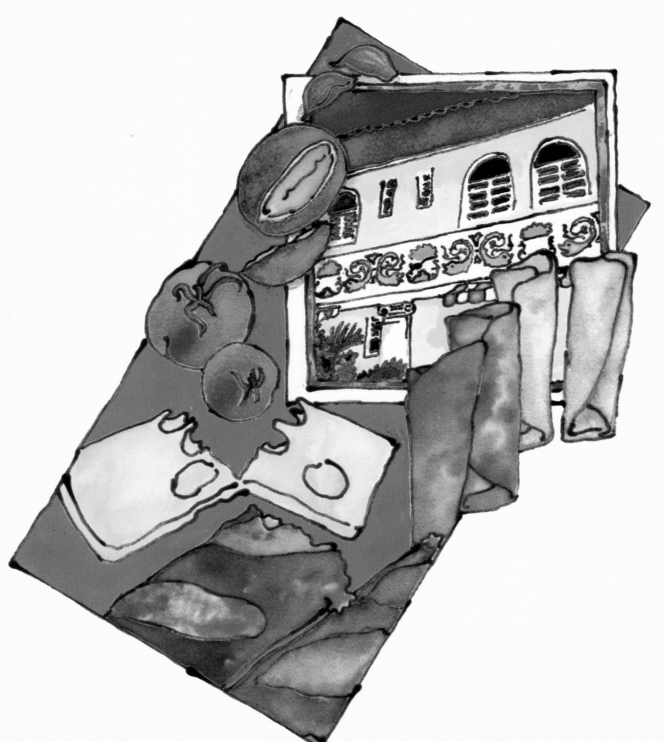

Appetizers & Snack

LOBSTER-MANGO CHUTNEY

The subtle sweetness of lobster and mango pair beautifully with hints of spiciness and tartness in the vinaigrette dressing in this dish.

Serves 4

- one 10-oz can lobster, drained and torn into ½-inch pieces and then chilled
- 1 cup thinly sliced celery
- 4 cups chopped mango, fresh or canned, drained and chilled
- ½ cup Curry-Lime Vinaigrette (page 39)
- 4 romaine, red leaf, Boston or bibb lettuce leaves
- 4 tsp thinly sliced scallions for garnish

Just before serving, toss lobster, celery, 2 cups mango chunks and Curry-Lime Vinaigrette together. Mound remaining mango chunks in center of lettuce-lined plates and top with lobster-mango mixture. Garnish, if desired, and serve.

CAVIAR PIE

This is a dazzling appetizer created by Mark Militello, one of Miami's premier chefs and owner of Mark's Place restaurant. While Militello is well known for his many dishes featuring tropical ingredients, he also shows that old favorites such as caviar will never go out of fashion.

Serves 4 – 6

- 1 onion, finely chopped
- 4 hard-cooked eggs, finely chopped
- one 8-oz container sour cream
- 1 oz American sturgeon caviar
- 1 oz salmon roe
- 1 oz black lumpfish roe
- 1 oz red lumpfish roe
- lime wedges and toast points for garnish

Twist chopped onion in a piece of cheesecloth to wring out bitter juices. Place onion on the bottom of a 9- or 10-inch ceramic dish. Arrange eggs on top of onion, pressing gently with the back of a spoon. Spoon sour cream over top. (Recipe can be prepared up to a day ahead to this stage.)

Just before serving, arrange the caviar circles or wedges atop sour cream. Garnish with lime wedges and toast points.

SMOKED MARLIN SPREAD

Here is another dish that has made its way from Key West to Miami and beyond. I like to serve this on toast points with cocktails at dinner parties. It can be made the day before and is no-muss, no-fuss.

Serves 4

- 8 oz smoked marlin
- ¼ cup sweet pickle relish
- 2 tbsp prepared horseradish
- 2 tbsp chopped onion
- ¼ tsp fresh-squeezed lime juice
- ½ tsp hot-pepper sauce or to taste
- up to ⅓ cup mayonnaise
- salt and fresh-ground pepper to taste

Coarsely chop fish and place in a mixing bowl. Add relish, horseradish, onion and lime juice and mix well. Add half the hot-pepper sauce and half the mayonnaise. Blend together and taste. Add more hot-pepper sauce according to your taste. Add salt and pepper to taste. The spread should be quite thick. Add more mayonnaise only if needed.

RIGHT
SMOKED MARLIN SPREAD

BEEF FILLET ON FRENCH BREAD

This is a pretty party dish with riotously colorful Papaya-Mango Salsa (page 28) resting atop garlicky roast beef. Pair with a cold soup in summer or a warm one in winter for an elegant meal.

Serves 4–6

- 3 lb fillet of beef
- ½ tbsp corn oil
- 1 clove garlic
- salt and fresh-ground black pepper to taste
- 1 loaf French bread

- 2 tbsp Citrus-Parsley Butter Log (page 50), brought to room temperature
- 2 cups Papaya-Mango Salsa (page 28)
- fresh parsley or cilantro for garnish

Preheat oven to 450°F. Remove all fat from the fillet and brush with the oil. Cut the garlic in half and rub fillet with it on all sides. Sprinkle with salt and pepper. Place in a roasting pan on a rack and roast 15 minutes. Turn oven down to 350°F and roast 15 more minutes for rare meat. Remove from oven and let rest at least 20 minutes before carving, or cool and then wrap and place in the refrigerator overnight.

Thinly slice while cold. Slice French bread into ½-inch pieces and butter 1 side with Citrus-Parsley Butter. Top the fillet slices and a small spoonful of Papaya-Mango Salsa. Place on a tray or serving platter and garnish with fresh cilantro or parsley.

SHRIMP-CHORIZO FAJITAS In LETTUCE

Serve these tempting tidbits at your next party, along with Curry-Lime Vinaigrette (page 39), No-Cook Mojito (page 40) or any of the chutneys in the first chapter.

Serves 4

- 8 oz chorizo, casing removed and finely diced
- ½ green bell pepper, seeded and diced
- 1½ tsp olive oil
- ½ sweet red pepper, seeded and diced

- 8 oz medium raw shrimp, shelled, deveined and diced
- 20 radicchio leaves
- 20 stuffed green olives for garnish (optional)

In a large skillet over medium heat, sauté sausage and green and red peppers in oil until peppers are tender, 8 minutes. Stir in shrimp and sauté 2 more minutes or until shrimp is no longer translucent.

Spoon about 2 tbsp shrimp-chorizo mixture into each radicchio leaf, then roll leaf and fasten with an olive-studded cocktail toothpick. Serve at once.

RIGHT
SHRIMP-CHORIZO FAJITAS IN LETTUCE

RIGHT It isn't surprising that houses so influenced by Spanish architecture are found in Española Way, Miami.

NUTTY RICKY RICARDO CHICKEN WINGS

These are great to serve with cocktails since the guests do not have to deal with a messy dipping sauce.

Serves 4

- 12 chicken wings or chicken wing drumettes
- salt and fresh-ground black pepper to taste
- 2 tbsp creamy peanut butter
- 2 tbsp soy sauce
- 1½ tbsp honey
- ½ tsp ground cumin
- 1 clove garlic, minced

- ¼–½ tsp dried hot red-pepper flakes to taste, or ½ fresh or canned jalapeño pepper, seeded and finely minced
- ⅓ cup finely chopped salted or unsalted roasted peanuts
- ¼ cup finely chopped fresh cilantro

Preheat oven to 400°F. In a shallow baking pan lined with foil, season chicken wings or drumettes with salt and pepper. Bake in middle of oven for 30 minutes, or until they begin to turn brown and become crisp.

While chicken wings are baking, in a small saucepan, stir together peanut butter, soy sauce, honey, cumin, garlic and pepper flakes. Cook over low heat, stirring until smooth. Brush chicken wings generously with sauce and bake them for 10–15 more minutes. Sprinkle chicken wings immediately with chopped peanuts and cilantro and let them cool slightly before serving.

SANDWICHES NUEVO CUBANO

One of South Florida's most popular snacks goes uptown and jazzy in this rendition that substitutes Mango Mustard (page 37) rather than the usual condiments of mustard and mayonnaise or butter. Add some salami to the cold cuts, if you like. When it comes to the meats in this sandwich, the more the merrier.

Slice loaf in half lengthwise and spread both halves with Mango Mustard. Layer with alternating slices of ham, pork and cheese. Place both halves under the broiler until unfilled half is slightly toasted. Remove from heat and add tomatoes, pickles and lettuce to half with the meat and cheese on it. Top with other half and cut into 4 sandwiches.

Serves 4

- 1 large loaf French bread
- ¼ cup Mango Mustard (page 37)
- 1 lb smoked ham, thinly sliced
- 1 lb roast pork, thinly sliced
- 8 oz Swiss cheese, cut into narrow ¼-inch strips
- tomatoes, thinly sliced
- dill pickles, thinly sliced
- 3 cups shredded Iceberg lettuce

CODFISH FRITTERS

In Miami, these are served with Simple Garlicky Aïoli, while in old Havana, folks sprinkled them with lime juice and enjoyed them with cocktails. You can have your cocktail in your dip if you eat them with Vodka Dip (page 35).

Serves 4
(makes about 1 dozen)

- 5 oz salt cod, submerged in bowl of water, covered and refrigerated for 24 hours with several changes of water to remove salt
- 1½ potatoes, peeled and diced
- 1 small egg
- 1 tbsp butter
- ⅛ tsp fresh-ground black pepper
- vegetable oil for frying

Cover cod and potatoes with water in a heavy-bottomed pan and cook until potatoes are tender. Drain and allow to cool. Shred cod with fingers to make certain all bones are removed and discarded. Mix shredded cod with potatoes, egg, butter and black pepper.

Fill large heavy skillet or deep fryer with 2–3 inches oil. Heat oil to 375°F. Drop batter a soupspoonful at a time into the oil without crowding the pan. If fritters bob to the top of the oil, submerge with tongs or a slotted metal spoon. Remove from oil when golden-brown all over. Drain on paper towels and serve immediately.

SMOKED GROUPER SPREAD

Grouper spread is popular at many pubs in South Florida where it is usually eaten on crackers. It also makes a nifty dip for crudités, too. Any white-fleshed fillet, such as halibut, whitefish or snapper, can be substituted or, in a pinch, use drained canned pink salmon.

Serves 4

- 7 oz cooked grouper, any bones or skin removed
- 8 oz cream cheese, softened
- 1 tbsp fresh-squeezed lime juice
- 1 tbsp grated onion
- 1 tsp prepared horseradish
- ¼ tsp Liquid Smoke
- ½ cup chopped walnuts
- 3 tbsp chopped fresh parsley or cilantro

In a blender or food processor, combine grouper, cream cheese, lime juice, onion, horseradish and liquid smoke. Process until smooth. Stir in walnuts and parsley or cilantro. Transfer to a crock or heavy small bowl. Cover and refrigerate until ready to serve.

RIGHT
SMOKED GROUPER SPREAD

SKIRT STEAK FAJITAS

Fajitas means, literally, "little thin belts." It seems that in the old days, along the borders of Mexico and Texas, every cut of beef was utilized to feed ranch hands and cattle drivers, including the tough skirt steak, which was cut into narrow strips and marinated to tenderize it. The *fajitas* were then grilled and wrapped into soft flour tortillas.

This is my variation of a dish I first encountered at the trend-setting, elegant Louie's Back Yard in Key West. Serve these with Tomato-Ginger Chutney (page 42) for unforgettable finger food. Use crisp lettuce leaves to roll this dish in instead of tortillas for a change of pace.

Serves 4

- 2½ cups No-Cook Mojito (page 40)
- ¼ cup Dijon mustard
- ¼ cup soy sauce
- salt and fresh-ground black pepper to taste
- 1 lb skirt steak, trimmed and cut into thin slices
- 2 tbsp olive oil
- 12 flour tortillas, warmed
- 2 cups Tomato-Ginger Chutney (page 42)
- sour cream (optional)
- lime wedges and cilantro for garnish (optional)

Combine Mojito, mustard, soy sauce, salt and pepper to make marinade. Add steak to marinade, turning it to coat it well, and leave to marinate in the refrigerator overnight.

Drain and discard marinade. In a large nonstick skillet, heat oil. Add steak, cook, turning frequently, until done to taste, 4–5 minutes. Remove from skillet.

Stuff tortillas with pieces of the steak topped with Tomato-Ginger Chutney and sour cream, if desired. Serve garnished with lime wedges and cilantro, if desired.

BELOW The ornate gardens at Vizcaya were very badly damaged by Hurricane Andrew in 1992.

62

MALANGA PANCAKES WITH CAVIAR

This is a Nuevo Cuban version of Beauty and the Beast. The "Beauty" is, of course, the caviar that festoons these pancakes. The "Beast" is the malanga, a homely tuber before it's peeled. Serve with Vodka Dip (page 35).

Serves 4

- 4 oz malanga or white potatoes, peeled and grated on large holes of grater
- 4 oz boniato or white potatoes, peeled and grated on large holes of grater
- 1 medium egg
- 1½ tbsp finely chopped fresh cilantro
- 1 clove garlic, minced
- ½ tsp fresh-squeezed lime juice
- ½ tsp salt
- 1 tbsp butter
- 1 tbsp vegetable oil
- 8 tbsp American sturgeon caviar

Note: If using white potatoes rather than malanga, add 1 tsp ground walnuts to the egg mixture. If using white potatoes instead of boniato, add ¼ tsp allspice to egg mixture.

Squeeze grated tubers in cheesecloth to remove water. In a bowl, beat egg, then stir in cilantro, garlic, lime juice and salt. Stir in grated tubers. Let stand 20 minutes at room temperature to congeal.

In a large skillet, heat butter and oil to moderate heat. Stir batter and divide into 4 small bowls or pitchers. In successions, pour half of the contents from each until you have formed 8 fairly uniform, 4-inch pancakes. Fry until golden brown for about 5 minutes, turning each pancake once.

Place pancakes on a warm platter, electric warming grill or warming tray and top each pancake with a thin layer of caviar, about 1 tbsp per pancake. Serve immediately.

CONCH FRITTERS

The fate of entire restaurants in Miami can rise or fall on the merits of their conch fritters, a spicy croquette that is the snack of first choice from the Florida Keys to Miami – soon to appear on your table too, I hope.

Serves 4

- 1 lb conch, abalone or squid, blanched and finely ground in a meat grinder or food processor
- 2 green bell peppers, seeded and finely sliced
- 2 small onions, finely diced
- 2 tsp baking powder
- 3 stalks celery, finely chopped
- 1 large egg
- 2 tsp chopped fresh cilantro
- ½ tsp cayenne pepper
- 2 tsp Worcestershire sauce
- 1 clove garlic, crushed
- pinch ground thyme
- ¼ tsp fresh-ground black pepper
- pinch baking soda
- 1 cup milk
- 1½ cups sifted all-purpose flour
- vegetable oil for deep frying

Mix together conch or substitute, peppers, onions, baking powder, celery, egg, cilantro, cayenne, Worcestershire, garlic, thyme, black pepper, baking soda and milk. Slowly stir in flour, then cover and refrigerate overnight.

In a deep, heavy saucepan, Dutch oven or deep fryer, heat oil 2–3 inches deep to 350°F. Drop soupspoonfuls of mix into oil without crowding pan. If fritters bob to top of oil, submerge with tongs or a slotted spoon. Remove from oil with same utensil when golden-brown on all sides. Drain on paper towels and serve immediately.

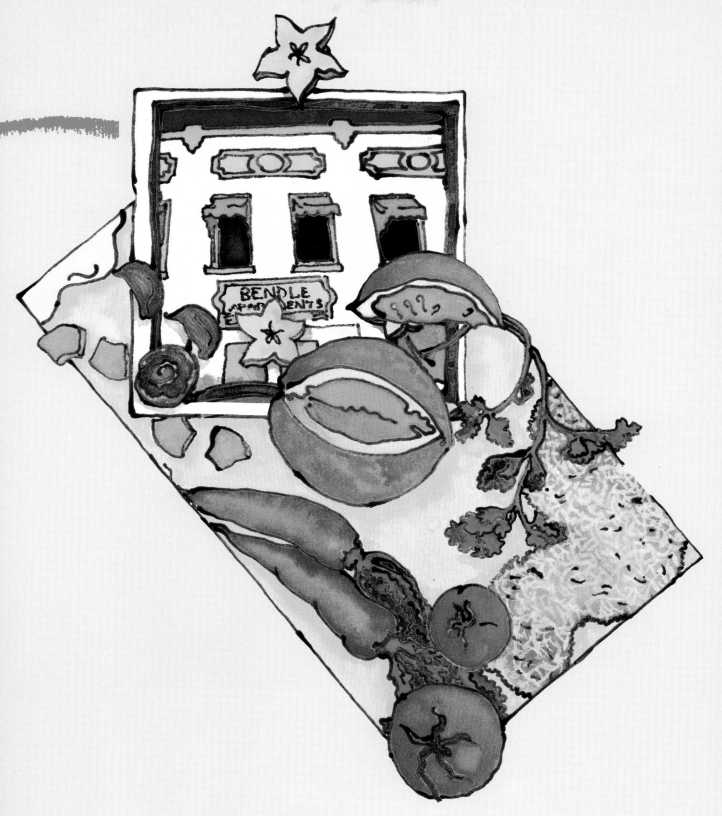

Salads

FRUITED CRAB SALAD

Surimi works quite well in this salad because when served cold in a no-cook dish, the pollack-paste based dish is indistinguishable from more expensive crabmeat. Of course, if you prefer to use real crabmeat, by all means do so.

If using fresh pineapple, cut lengthwise into quarters, cutting through crown, remove fruit from shells, discard core and reserve shells to use as "pineapple boats."

Serves 4

- 1 large fresh pineapple, or 16-oz can unsweetened pineapple, cut into bite-sized chunks, drained
- 2 lb crabmeat, cut into chunks, or surimi (flake or chunk style)
- 1 large mango, peeled and cubed
- 1½ cups honeydew melon balls
- 2 cups seedless grapes
- yogurt or sour cream to serve (optional)

Combine pineapple, crabmeat or surimi, mango, honeydew melon balls and grapes. Place in your pineapple boats or in a glass bowl. Chill until ready to serve. Serve with yogurt or sour cream, if desired.

ENSALADA DE MOROS Y CRISTIANOS

When Cubans serve black beans and rice together, they call it *Moros y Cristianos* – Moors and Christians – after the Saracens who invaded Christian Spain in the 8th Century AD. This is a cold version of the dish. Garnish with a dollop of Delicato Mango Salsa (page 30) if you like.

Serves 4–6

- 2 cups cooked or canned black beans, rinsed and drained, if canned
- 2 cups cooked white rice
- 1½ cups chopped fresh cilantro, loosely packed
- ¼ cup fresh-squeezed lime juice
- ¾ cup olive oil
- ½ cup chopped onion
- 2 cloves garlic, chopped
- salt and fresh-ground pepper to taste

In a bowl mix together beans, rice and cilantro. Place lime juice in a small bowl and whisk in oil. Add onion and garlic and then toss with beans. Add salt and pepper to taste.

PINK COLESLAW

If you are unable to find the small Key limes for this refreshing slaw, substitute the juice of a regular lime and reduce the sugar by 1 tsp. If you're watching your weight or cholesterol, use fat-free mayonnaise.

Serves 4–6

- ½ head green cabbage, rinsed and drained
- 2 carrots, peeled
- 1 small onion
- 2 tbsp corn oil
- 2 pink grapefruits, peeled, pith removed and cut into sections
- 2 tbsp fresh-squeezed Key or Persian lime juice
- 4 tsp sugar (3 tsp if using Persian lime juice)
- 4 tbsp mayonnaise
- 2 tsp Dijon mustard
- salt and fresh-ground black pepper to taste

Thinly slice cabbage, carrots and onion in a food processor or by hand. Place in a bowl and toss with oil. Mix grapefruit sections in the lime juice and sugar and add to sliced vegetables. Add mayonnaise and mustard and toss well. Add salt and pepper. Toss again before serving.

CHICKEN MANGO SALAD

If you like cheddar with apples or other fruit, you'll love it with mango and chicken. The Ginger-Orange Mayo (page 32) pulls this symphony of tastes and textures together.

Serves 4

- 3 cups fresh-chopped mango, or 12-oz can unsweetened mango, drained and cut into bite-size chunks
- 2 cups diced cooked chicken
- 4 oz cheddar cheese, cut into thin strips

- ½ cup sliced celery
- ½ cup plus 4 tsp finely chopped scallions
- 1½ cups Ginger-Orange Mayo (page 32)
- 4 cups romaine, bibb, Boston or red leaf (or combination) leaves, rinsed and torn

In a large mixing bowl, combine mango, chicken, cheese, celery, ½ cup scallions and Ginger-Orange Mayo and toss gently. Place salad on lettuce-lined dishes and garnish with reserved scallions.

PASSION FRUIT CUP

This recipe is from J. R. Brooks & Son of Homestead, Florida, one of the foremost growers of tropical fruits and vegetables in the country.

Serves 4

- 4 passion fruit, tops cut and pulp scooped out
- 1 banana, sliced
- 1 large kiwi, peeled, halved and cut into semi-circles
- 2 tbsp honey
- 1 cup seedless red grapes, halved
- squirt of juice from 1 Key, Persian or regular lime

Combine fruits with honey. Add 1–2 squeezes lime juice to taste, and serve.

Soups

WHITE BEAN & YUCA VICHYSSOISE

Toss some leftover bits of chorizo, ham or flank steak into this concoction after it's puréed and you have a Nuevo version of Galician Bean Soup, so beloved by Cubans. I prefer this potage to the authentic, which contains turnip, collard or mustard greens and none of the gentle seasoning.

Serves 4–6

- 2 tbsp plus 2 tsp olive oil, divided
- 4 tsp white wine
- 4 cloves garlic, crushed
- 2 tbsp butter or margarine
- 2 leeks, sliced and rinsed
- 2 stalks celery, sliced
- two 19-oz cans cannellini (white kidney) beans, drained and rinsed
- 1 lb yuca or potatoes, peeled and cut into 2-inch sections
- two 14½-oz cans chicken broth
- 2 tsp chopped fresh rosemary
- 2 tsp chopped fresh thyme leaves
- 2 tsp chopped fresh sage
- 2 bay leaves
- salt and fresh-ground white pepper to taste
- 2 tbsp snipped fresh chives for garnish (optional)

In a small skillet, heat 2 tsp olive oil and white wine. Add garlic and sauté over a low flame about 10 minutes.

Meanwhile, heat remaining olive oil and butter in a large saucepan. Add leeks and celery, and sauté until wilted, about 10 minutes. Add beans and yuca to the leeks with the chicken stock, herbs and bay leaves. Add garlic mixture and simmer until yuca is soft, about 30 minutes. Remove bay leaves. Add salt and pepper to a taste. Purée in a blender or food processor. Garnish and serve.

SHERRIED LOBSTER BISQUE

This is a rich, delectable soup. I like to use angler-fish, commonly called monkfish, because it tastes a lot like more expensive Maine lobster when cooked in this dish. But any firm-fleshed fish, such as redfish, red snapper, tilefish, catfish or cod, will do. Pair this soup with a green salad and some crusty bread and you have a memorable meal.

Serves 4–6

- 3 tbsp butter
- 10–12 stalks celery, chopped
- 1 onion, chopped
- ¼ tsp dried thyme
- ½ tsp red-pepper flakes
- 1 tbsp fresh lemon peel slivers
- 3 tbsp all-purpose flour
- 1 cup canned chicken broth
- 1 cup milk
- 2 tbsp dry sherry
- 1 lb lobster meat or substitute (see above)
- salt and fresh-ground white pepper to taste
- 1 tbsp red bell pepper slivers for garnish
- pinch paprika for garnish
- oyster crackers to serve

In a large saucepan, melt butter. Add celery, onion, thyme, pepper flakes and lemon peel. Cook until vegetables are softened, stirring once more, about 20 minutes. Stir in flour a little at a time. Gradually stir in broth and milk. Cover and simmer until bubbling and thick, stirring occasionally, about 5–10 minutes.

Add seafood or fish, cover and cook until fish is opaque, about 5 minutes. Season with sherry, salt and pepper. Garnish with pepper slivers and paprika. Serve topped with oyster crackers.

WHITE GAZPACHO

Serves 4–6

- 3 seedless cucumbers, peeled and chopped
- 3 cloves garlic, minced
- 3 cups chicken stock
- 2 tbsp mild vinegar or lime juice
- 2 cups buttermilk
- ¼ cup chopped scallions
- ¼ cup chopped fresh dill
- chive flowers for garnish (optional)

In a large bowl, combine cucumbers, garlic, stock, vinegar or lime juice, buttermilk, scallions and dill. Cover and chill in the refrigerator overnight to allow flavors to mellow.

Stir the soup thoroughly and garnish with chive flowers before serving.

BELOW The Miami skyline at dusk.

RED GAZPACHO

I prefer to chop vegetables by hand for gazpacho because I like my soup thick, not puréed. While it takes a little longer to do it this way, another benefit is that you can serve the vegetables separately from the soup and let your family or guests spoon in the items they want. Tortilla chips make wonderful "crackers" for serving with gazpacho.

Serves 4–6

- 2 cups tomato juice
- 2 tbsp olive oil
- ¾ tsp chili powder
- ¼ Bermuda onion, quartered and finely chopped
- 1 small cucumber, peeled, seeded and finely chopped
- 2 small green bell peppers, seeded and finely chopped
- 3 medium to large tomatoes, finely chopped
- 2 large cloves garlic, crushed
- salt and fresh-ground black pepper to taste

In a blender or food processor combine tomato juice, olive oil and chili powder. Whirl until liquid is well blended. (Chill at this point if you do not want to serve the soup already mixed.)

In a large bowl, combine tomato juice mixture and chopped vegetables. Chill until ready to serve. Season with salt and pepper just before serving.

RIGHT
RED GAZPACHO

SPLIT-PEA SOUP WITH CHORIZO

The chorizo in this classic gives the soup a Nuevo twist. The concoction, along with just about any of the appetizers in this book, makes a spectacular lunch for company.

Serves 4–6

- 1½ lb cured chorizo, casing removed, thinly sliced
- 1 onion, chopped
- 1 rib celery, finely chopped
- 2 cloves garlic, minced
- 1 lb split peas, picked over
- 4 cups canned chicken broth
- 4 cups water
- ½ tsp dried thyme
- 1 bay leaf
- 3 carrots, halved lengthwise, and thinly sliced crosswise
- salt and fresh-ground black pepper
- croutons for garnish

In a heavy-bottomed saucepan over moderate heat, brown chorizo, stirring constantly. Transfer with a slotted spoon to paper towels to drain, and pour off all but 1 tbsp fat. In remaining fat, cook onion, celery and garlic over moderately low heat, stirring until celery is softened. Then add split peas, broth, water, thyme and bay leaf, and simmer, covered, stirring occasionally for 1¼ hours.

Stir in carrots and simmer, covered, until carrots are tender, 30–35 minutes. Discard bay leaf, add the cooked chorizo, season with salt and pepper, and serve soup with croutons.

MANGO SOUP

The secret of this refreshing concoction is the seltzer and the extracts which enhance the flavors of the tropical fruits. Serve in small soup bowls set in larger bowls lined with crushed ice – or serve in frosty glass mugs.

Serves 4–6

- 1 small mango, peeled and cut into chunks
- 3 star fruit, 2 cut into small pieces and 1 sliced for garnish
- ⅛ medium pineapple, peeled
- ½ cup lemon-lime seltzer, or soda pop
- ⅓ cup apricot nectar or juice
- 2 tsp fresh-squeezed lime juice
- 1 tsp pineapple extract
- fresh mint leaves for garnish (optional)

In blender or food processor, purée mango, star fruit and pineapple until smooth. With motor running, add seltzer or soda, apricot nectar or juice, lime juice and pineapple extract. Process until blended. Cover and chill until ready to serve.

Float a star fruit slice in each serving and garnish with mint leaves, if desired.

BLACK BEAN SOUP

Just as no two snowflakes are alike in colder climes, no two black bean soups are identical in Miami. This recipe is my slight variation of the soup served at Yuca, a restaurant in Coral Gables, Florida – a popular place whose name is a play on words: yuca is a tropical tuber, the "spud" of the Caribbean, and yuca is also an acronym for "young upscale Cuban-Americans."

This thick, velvety potion is a meal when served with a crisp salad and garlic bread. To give it a party flair, serve it over Herbed Rice Cakes (page 108) and garnish with a dollop of sour cream sprinkled with fine chopped green onions.

Serves 4–6

- 1 lb dried black beans
- 3 quarts water
- 2 bay leaves
- ½ cup olive oil
- 1 large sweet red pepper, seeded and coarsely diced
- 1 large green pepper, seeded and coarsely diced
- 3 small shallots, diced
- 1½ tbsp sugar
- 2 tbsp chopped fresh parsley or cilantro
- 2 cups No-Cook Majito (page 40)

Soak the beans in the water overnight in a large, heavy-bottomed pot.

Next day, add bay leaves to the beans and water and bring mixture to a boil. Reduce heat to simmer and cook, uncovered, over low heat for 3–4 hours, until tender. Stir occasionally and add more water if necessary.

Heat a large, heavy-bottomed skillet. Add olive oil and sauté the red and green peppers and shallots until tender. Add the sugar, then add the parsley or cilantro and sauté 30 seconds more. Remove the bay leaves and stir the sautéed mixture and No-Cook Mojito into the soup just before serving.

BELOW Bright pink colors and Art Deco style are a feature of Florida – seen here in Key West.

Fish & Seafood

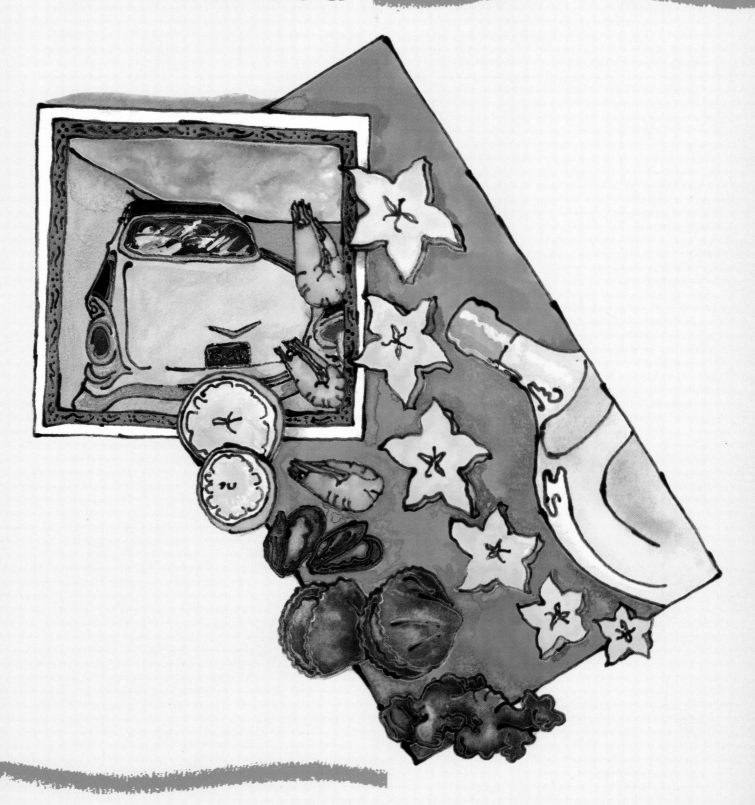

CRAB CAKES

Nothing tastes better than these zesty cakes topped with Simple Garlicky Aioli (page 32), Pepper-Lime Dip (page 33) or Mango Mustard (page 37). Add a salad plus corn on the cob or Mia-Mex Star Fruit & Black Bean Salsa (page 27) in summer or Corn Cubana (page 107) in winter and dig in.

Serves 4

- 1 lb lump crabmeat
- 5 saltines (or 10 wafers), crumbled in blender
- 2 eggs, beaten
- ½ cup finely chopped fresh parsley
- 1 tsp Worcestershire sauce
- 2–3 tbsp mayonnaise and/or Dijon mustard
- vegetable oil for frying
- clarified butter or ghee or frying in skillet or vegetable oil for deep frying
- salt and fresh-ground pepper to taste

Remove any shell or cartilage from crabmeat. Mix all ingredients except butter or oil together gently but thoroughly with a fork. Refrigerate 1 hour for easier handling, then mold into patties.

Place a thin layer of clarified butter or ghee in the bottom of a skillet large enough to hold all 4 patties one-layer deep. Heat skillet over medium high heat until sizzling hot. Fry patties until golden brown on one side and then turn with slotted spatula and fry until golden brown on other side. Remove with spatula and drain on paper towels. Serve immediately. Alternately, heat oil 3 inches deep in a heavy pan, Dutch oven, or deep fryer to 325°F and fry submerged in hot oil until golden brown on both sides. Do not crowd pan and if patties bob to top of oil, submerge with tongs or a slotted metal spoon. Remove from oil with the same utensil when golden brown. Drain on paper towels and serve immediately.

SEAFOOD LINGUINE

Miami Cubans have embraced pasta with almost as much passion as their fellow Latins, the Italians. One popular restaurant is even called Lotsa Pasta. Here is a dish served by a popular seafood chain in South Florida called Shells. Pair it with a green salad and Key Lime Pie (page 14) and, if it's a warm, humid day, you'll feel like you're in Florida.

Pasta:
- 1 lb linguine
- 2 tsp butter

Seafood mix:
- 4 oz mussel meat
- 6 oz chopped cooked and drained clams
- 10 oz raw scallops
- 12 oz shelled raw shrimp

Sauce:
- ½ cup olive oil
- ½ cup dry white wine
- 8 cloves garlic, finely chopped
- salt and fresh-ground white pepper to taste
- 2 dashes soy sauce
- 2 cups heavy cream

Cook the linguine with the butter in salted boiling water until *al dente*. Drain and set aside.

To make the sauce, in a large saucepan, combine olive oil, wine, garlic, salt and pepper, soy sauce and heavy cream. Bring to a boil, stirring over medium-high heat.

Add seafood, stir, then add the cooked linguine. Stir gently and cook over medium heat until seafood is cooked through and dish has a creamy consistency, about 10 minutes. Serve immediately.

FISH & SEAFOOD SHOPPING TIP:
Give the sniff, sight and touch tests. If it smells like ammonia, don't buy it. Look for browning or drying out around the edges of fillets, too, and avoid those as well. If you're buying a whole fish, ask the fishmonger to touch it – it should spring back if it's not old and mushy. When clams, oysters and mussels are tapped, they should close tightly.

GRILLED MOJITO SHRIMP-MANGO KEBABS

These kebabs evoke a multicultural theme stretching from Cuba to Baja to the Pacific Rim. I like to dip the kebabs in Papaya-Mango Salsa (page 28).

- 1 cup No-Cook Mojito (page 40)
- 1 tsp ground achiote seeds or paprika
- 1 tsp chili powder
- 1 tbsp molasses
- 3 large slightly green mangoes or green tomatoes, seeded and peeled

- 2 large onions
- 36 medium raw shrimp, about 2 lb, shelled and deveined
- salt and fresh-ground black pepper to taste

In a small saucepan, combine Mojito, achiote seeds, chili powder and molasses. Bring to a boil, then simmer over low heat, 5 minutes. Remove from heat and set aside.

Cut mangoes or tomatoes and onions into chunks about ¼ inch in diameter. Thread onto skewers alternately with the shrimp. Allow the coals to heat to medium (300°F–350°F).

Brush grill rack with oil to prevent the food from sticking. Grill until the shrimp are just opaque, 3–4 minutes per side. Just before you remove skewers from grill, brush both sides generously with the glaze. Leave the skewers over the fire just long enough for the glaze to color, then pull them off and serve.

CITRUS-CRUSTED SHRIMP
WITH GINGER STAR FRUIT AND RUM

This is a creation of Allen Susser of Chef Allen's, his restaurant in Miami. If you do not care for a rum flavor, substitute lime juice. Enjoy with Yuca Fries (page 110) or Plantain Rounds with Brie (page 112).

Serves 4

- grated zest and juice of 2 lemons
- grated zest and juice of 2 limes
- 1 jalapeño pepper, seeded and diced
- 1 tbsp white peppercorns, crushed
- 1 tbsp coarse salt
- 2 tbsp brown sugar
- 1 tbsp olive oil
- 12 large raw shrimp, shelled, deveined and butterflied
- olive oil for sautéeing
- 2 star fruit, sliced crosswise
- 2 tsp sliced fresh ginger root
- ¼ cup rum or lime juice

Combine lime and lemon zest, jalapeño pepper, and peppercorns and set aside. In a small saucepan, simmer the lemon and lime juice and brown sugar until 3 tablespoons are left. Add salt and zest mixture. Cook for 1 minute more and remove from heat. Moisten with 1 tablespoon olive oil and let cool.

Press mixture onto both sides of butterflied shrimp, then sauté in hot olive oil. Cook for 1 minute, then add star fruit and ginger. Add rum, swirl it around in pan for a few seconds and serve immediately.

LEMON-SCENTED POMPANO ON SPINACH AND LEEKS

Pompano, a renowned Florida fish, is worth some pomp and circumstance. Considered a delicacy even in Florida, it may be hard to find. Substitute any firm-fleshed, thin white fish or sea scallops. This slightly Oriental rendition pairs nicely with Gingery Jasmine Rice (page 118), Chayote and Carrots (page 114), and Passion Fruit Cup (page 70).

Serves 4

- 1 small lemon, thinly sliced
- 1 small lime, thinly sliced
- 6 bay leaves
- 1½ cups water
- 1 large leek, split, thinly sliced crosswise and rinsed
- 1 lb spinach or Swiss chard, stems removed
- ½ lb pompano fillets or substitute (see above)
- 1 tsp mild soy sauce
- fresh-ground black pepper

In a steamer, combine lemon, lime, bay leaves and water. Cover and simmer over low heat 2 minutes. Bring liquid to a boil over high heat. Spread sliced leeks one layer thick in steamer basket. Cover and steam until tender, about 3 minutes. Uncover, pack in all the spinach, cover and steam, stirring once, until wilted, about 4 minutes. Transfer steamer basket to the sink and press spinach–leek mixture very lightly to extract excess moisture.

Transfer spinach–leek mixture to a large skillet and set aside on the stovetop. Return water with lemon, lime and bay leaves to a boil over high heat. Lay the fish fillets in steamer basket, cover and steam until the fish are just cooked through and flake easily if tested with tip of knife, 3–4 minutes. Quickly reheat spinach over high heat, sprinkling soy sauce on top and tossing, about 1 minute.

To serve, arrange spinach and fish on 4 warm plates. Season fish with pepper to taste.

CILANTRO-LIME GRILLED TUNA

This simple but elegant treatment of everyone's favorite – tuna – tastes great with Lime-Pepper Noodles (page 110) and Passion Fruit Cup (page 70).

Serves 4

- ¼ cup olive oil
- 3 tbsp fresh-squeezed lime juice
- ½ cup chopped fresh cilantro
- ½ tsp salt
- ¼ tsp fresh-ground black pepper
- 2 lb tuna steaks
- extra oil for broiler rack

In shallow medium glass baking dish, stir together oil, lime juice, cilantro, salt and pepper. Add tuna to marinade; turn to coat. Cover with plastic wrap and, refrigerate 1 hour, turning once.

Preheat broiler. Lightly grease broiler rack. Broil steaks 6 inches from heat 3–4 minutes. Brush with marinade, turn steaks over and broil 3–4 more minutes or until flakes when tested with fork.

BELOW "Fresh fish" in Miami often means it was caught only a few hours earlier.

PECAN-ENCRUSTED FLOUNDER

If you don't wish to finish this crunchy delight with a butter sauce, skip that step and douse, Cuban-style, with No-Cook Mojito (page 40) or top with Simple Garlicky Aioli (page 32) or Sweet & Sassy Mangolade (page 34) – the possibilities are endless. Any way you finish the dish, it tastes like a wonderful combination of Cuba and Old South when paired with So-Sweet Sweet Potatoes & Carrots (page 109).

Serves 4

- salt and fresh-ground pepper to taste
- 8 small flounder fillets, about 8 oz total, skinned
- 1 large egg
- 3 tbsp water
- 2 tsp dark soy sauce
- ¾ cup pecans, finely chopped
- 3 tbsp vegetable oil
- 2 tbsp olive oil (optional)
- 3 tbsp chopped fresh cilantro or parsley for garnish (optional)
- 2 tbsp Tango-Mango Butter Log, butter or margarine (optional)
- 1 tbsp fresh-squeezed lime juice (optional)

Salt and pepper both sides of fillets. Whisk egg, water and soy sauce together in a large bowl. Dip fillets, one at a time, in the egg mixture to coat lightly, then dredge evenly in nuts. In a large nonstick skillet over medium-high heat, heat 1 tbsp of the vegetable oil. When hot, add as many fillets as will fit without crowding. Sauté for a total of about 2 minutes, or until lightly browned on both sides. Add more oil, if needed. Garnish and serve fillets.

If you wish to serve Tango-Mango Butter over the fillets, transfer fillets to a warm serving plate or platter and wipe skillet with paper towels. Add remaining olive oil and Tango-Mango Butter or butter or margarine. Cook until butter foams and starts to brown. Add lime juice, stir once, and then pour mixture over fish, garnish, and serve.

RIGHT
PECAN-ENCRUSTED FLOUNDER

JUICY SWORDFISH

Here's the perfect prepare-ahead, quick-cook dish. Serve with Pineapple Coconut Relish (page 31), which can be made ahead of time, and Gingery Jasmine Rice (page 118). Cap off the meal with No-Cook Rum Chiquitas (page 120).

Serves 4

- ⅔ cup No-Cook Mojito (page 40)
- 1 tbsp ground ginger
- 5 tbsp Madeira wine
- 4 swordfish steaks, 4–6 oz each

In a shallow glass dish, combine Mojito, ginger and Madeira. Marinate fish in mixture overnight.

Next day, grill or broil fish until it flakes easily when tested with tip of a knife, about 7 minutes, basting once or twice with leftover marinade. Serve immediately.

AN EASY WAY TO TEST YOUR GRILL:
If you don't have a flat surface oven thermometer, do the hand test: Place your hand at cooking height, just above the grill rack. If you can hold it there for 3–4 seconds, the heat is medium.

RED SNAPPER WITH CITRUS

Another of Florida's premier fishes is red snapper. If it's not available, substitute any white, firm-fleshed fish. This is a recipe that leans toward classic, but the citrus takes it out of the ordinary. Serve with Gingery Jasmine Rice (page 118) and Passion Fruit Cup (page 70).

Serves 4

- 1 tbsp olive oil
- 2 shallots, minced, or white part of 4 scallions, trimmed and thinly sliced
- 8 oz fresh mushrooms, trimmed and thinly sliced (3½ cups)
- ½ cup fresh-squeezed orange juice
- ½ cup bottled clam juice
- ½ tsp salt
- fresh-ground black pepper
- red snapper, perch, turbot or sole fillets, about 4 oz each
- ¼ cup minced fresh parsley

In large skillet over medium heat, heat oil. Add shallots and cook about 1 minute. Add mushrooms and cook 1 more minute to soften slightly. Add juices and bring to a boil. Cover and simmer gently until mushrooms are completely tender, 5–7 minutes. Uncover and boil over high heat until liquid is somewhat thickened, about 5 minutes. Season with half the salt and pepper to taste.

Place fish fillets over mushrooms. Sprinkle with remaining salt and pepper to taste. Reduce heat to medium low, cover and steam fillets until just opaque in center or flake easily when tested with the tip of a knife, 6–8 minutes. (Or bake, covered, at 350°F for 15 minutes.) Sprinkle fish with parsley and serve immediately.

CRISP OVEN-FRIED FLOUNDER

Jazz up this tastes-like-fried-but-it's-not, local preparation with Stoplight Salsa (page 29) or douse the fish at the table, Cuban-style, with No-Cook Mojito (page 40).

Other enticing ideas: top with Simple Garlicky Aioli (page 32) or Sweet & Sassy Mangolade (page 34). Serve with Black Bean Soup (page 34), a crisp salad and Key Lime Pie (page 123).

Serves 4

- 1 lb flounder fillets, thawed if frozen
- vegetable oil or cooking spray
- ½ cup fine dry bread crumbs
- ½ tsp paprika
- ¼ tsp onion powder
- ¼ tsp dried thyme leaves
- 1 large egg white
- 1 tbsp olive oil

Preheat oven to 450°F. Cut fish into 4 even portions. Line a cookie sheet with foil (for easy cleanup). Lightly coat foil with oil or vegetable cooking spray. Mix bread crumbs and seasonings. Beat egg white with fork in shallow bowl.

Dip fish in egg, then in crumbs to coat. Place in prepared pan. Drizzle evenly with olive oil. Bake until fish is opaque in center and flakes easily if tested with the tip of a knife, about 10 minutes.

RIGHT
SAUTÉED SNAPPER

SAUTÉED SNAPPER

Place this noble fish on a bed of Sweet & Sassy Mangolade (page 34) and top off with a dollop of Pineapple-Coconut Relish (page 31). Serve with favorite green side salad and dessert. If you can't find snapper, substitute any white, firm-fleshed fish, such as perch, turbot or sole.

Serves 4

- 4 snapper fillets, 6–8 oz each
- all-purpose flour
- salt and fresh-ground white pepper
- 1 stick Tango Mango Butter Log (page 49)

Lightly dust the snapper fillets with flour. Add salt and white pepper to taste.

In large skillet over medium-high heat, melt butter log. Place fillets into skillet and sauté until lightly browned, on both sides.

SHRIMP HASH CAKES

Allen Susser of Chef Allen's restaurant in Miami created this dish. He uses rock shrimp from Florida's coastal waters, but the dish is just as good if you use with any high-quality shrimp or prawns. Susser places the hash cake atop a thin potato pancake and encircles it with a piquant mustard sauce, but the cakes could also be placed atop Plantain-Apple Patties (page 114) and garnished with Sweet & Sassy Mangolade (page 34) or Mango Mustard (page 37).

In a large bowl, combine shrimp, tomato, chives, basil, brandy, cornstarch and cayenne. Mix well. Fold in grated potato. Stir in egg whites until evenly distributed, then let mixture stand 10 minutes.

Into a large skillet, pour ¼ inch of the olive oil. Add garlic and cook over a high heat 30 seconds, then discard garlic. Reduce heat to moderately high and when the oil begins to shimmer, scoop a scant ¼ cup of the hash mixture into skillet. Flatten slightly with the back of a spoon into a patty about 2½ inches in diameter. Form 4 more patties in the pan and fry, turning once with a spatula, until crisp, browned and the shrimp turn bright pink, 2–3 minutes per side. (Be careful when turning because the patties are fragile.)

Transfer hash cakes to paper towels to drain. Using a slotted spoon, remove any hash particles from the oil. If necessary, add enough oil to reach a ¼-inch depth and heat over moderately high heat. Form and fry remaining hash cakes.

Serves 4

- 8 oz raw or frozen and thawed rock shrimp, deveined and cut into ½-inch pieces
- 1 plum tomato, peeled, seeded and finely diced
- 3 tbsp snipped fresh chives
- 1 tbsp chopped fresh basil
- 1 tbsp brandy
- 2 tsp cornstarch
- ⅛ tsp cayenne pepper
- 1 large or 2 medium potatoes, baked, cooled, peeled and grated
- 3 egg whites, well beaten
- olive oil for frying
- 1 clove garlic
- Sweet & Sassy Mangolade (page 34) or Mango Mustard (page 37) (optional)

RIGHT Deep sea fishing is both a commercial activity and a sport in Miami.

NUTTY ROASTED RED SNAPPER

Deservedly, red snapper is one of the most sought after fishes and warrants a gorgeous presentation. To round out the meal, serve with a crisp salad and Gingery-Jasmine Rice (page 118).

Serves 4

- 1 tbsp olive oil
- 6 red snapper fillets, ½-inch thick each
- 2 tbsp clarified butter (see box)
- 1 tsp chopped fresh thyme leaves
- ⅛ tsp fresh-ground black pepper
- ⅛ tsp salt
- 1 cup Papaya-Mango Salsa (page 28) for garnish (optional)
- ½ cup toasted pumpkin seeds or almond slivers for garnish (optional)

Preheat oven to 500°F. Grease a jelly-roll pan with 1 tbsp olive oil and place fillets on pan. Brush fillets with 2 tbsp clarified butter, then sprinkle with thyme, pepper and salt. Bake 4 minutes.

If desired, spoon salsa in center of heated plates. Using wide spatula, place fillets on top and sprinkle with toasted pumpkin seeds or almond slivers.

ABOUT CLARIFIED BUTTER:
Also called "drawn butter" or "ghee," this is simply butter that has the milk solids removed so it tolerates high temperatures without burning. Place any amount in heavy pan over low heat. As butter melts and white solids curdle on surface, pour into a glass measuring cup. After a few minutes, the butter will separate into layers with the milk solids on the bottom. At this point, strain the clear yellow top layer into a lidded container. Will keep for weeks in refrigerator and can also be frozen.

MONKFISH IN BANANA LEAVES

The secret to this dish is the banana leaves, which keep moisture in and make for a dramatic looking dish. Serve this with Pepper-Lime Dip (page 33), Curried Almond Rice (page 117) and Catalan Creme Brulée (page 121).

Serves 4

- 2 tbsp olive oil
- ½ tsp paprika
- ¼ tsp fresh-ground black pepper
- 1 lb monkfish fillet, cut into twenty six 1-inch cubes
- 2–3 banana leaves, or ½ 17-oz jar grape leaves, rinsed

Mix olive oil, paprika and pepper together. Toss monkfish cubes in oil mixture to coat, then cover and refrigerate for several hours or overnight.

If using grape leaves, drain and pat them dry. Brush the banana or grape leaves lightly with oil remaining in the monkfish marinade, moistening with extra olive oil if necessary. Cut the leaves lengthwise into ½-inch-wide strips. Wrap each piece of monkfish with a strip of leaf and skewer through the leaf and fish together with a single piece of fish per skewer.

Lightly oil the grill rack, and grill the monkfish over medium high heat about 2 minutes per side. Line serving tray with leftover banana leaf strips in a basket weave pattern. If using grape leaves, dry remaining grape leaves and overlap on serving tray.

SALMON IN ROMAINE FAJITAS

This dish makes for a dramatic presentation, yet guests can handle these easily at a cocktail party or backyard barbecue. Serve with skewered grilled onion wedges and tomato halves and Pepper-Lime Dip (page 33).

Serves 4

- ⅔ cup No-Cook Mojito (page 19)
- 1 lb salmon fillets of even thickness, cut into 4 portions
- 2 tbsp vegetable oil
- grated zest of 1 lime
- ¼ tsp cayenne pepper
- 4 large romaine lettuce leaves, rinsed, dried and thick stems removed

Pour Mojito over salmon and marinate 15 minutes, turning salmon pieces at 5-minute intervals.

Arrange four 12-inch squares of foil on work surface and place lettuce leaf in center of each. Remove salmon, a piece at a time, from marinade; discard marinade. Place each salmon piece on a lettuce leaf and carefully wrap salmon in the leaves. Fold 2 opposite sides of each foil square over lettuce pocket in tight double fold and crimp ends tightly to seal. Place packets on hot grill rack.

Cook with grill covered until salmon is cooked through and flakes easily if tested with tip of knife, 15–18 minutes. Open packets carefully to avoid escaping steam; serve salmon in packets. (This can also be baked in an oven. Preheat oven to 400°F. Prepare packets as directed above and place on cookie sheet to bake 15–20 minutes.)

FISH & SEAFOOD COOKING TIP:
Canadian Guide: Measure fish at the thickest and allow 10 minutes cooking time, using any method, per inch of thickness. Double the cooking time if fish is frozen. Lift a flake and check thickest part; fish is done when it is just opaque (as opposed to translucent) and flakes easily if tested with the tip of a knife.

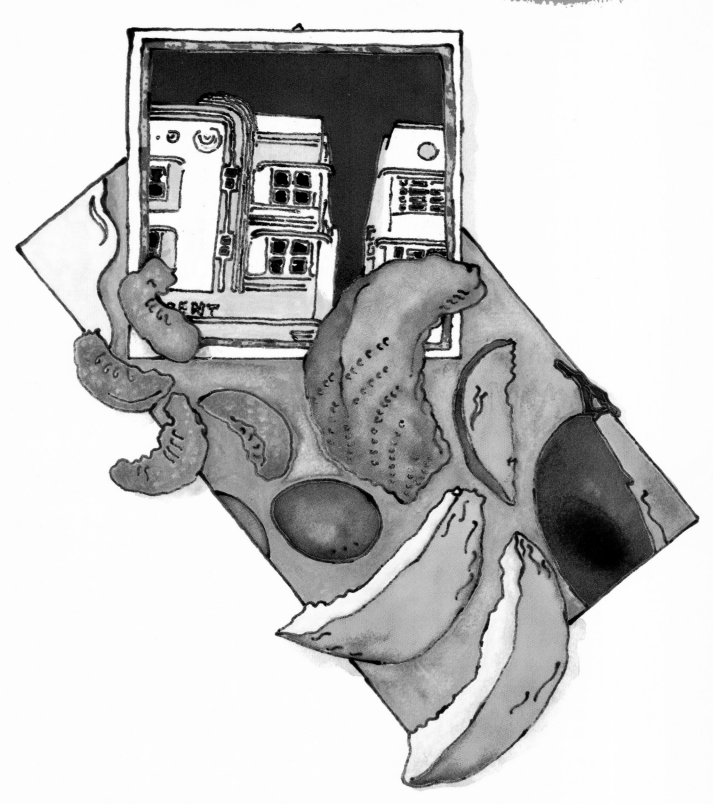

Poultry

PECAN-CRUSTED CHICKEN

To lend color to this dish, you can't beat a side dish of sweet potatoes or yams and a pretty dish of Pink Coleslaw (page 68). Garnish your serving platter with pink grapefruit sections and a few fresh mint or basil leaves.

Serves 4

- 2 cups milk
- 4 tsp cayenne pepper
- 4 skinned, boneless chicken breasts, trimmed of fat and tendon cut to flatten
- 1 tsp salt
- 2 tsp fresh-ground black pepper
- 2 cup cornmeal
- 4 egg whites, lightly beaten
- 2 cup pecans, coarsely chopped
- 4 tbsp clarified butter (page 91)
- 4 tbsp corn oil
- pink grapefruit sections for garnish (optional)
- fresh basil or mint leaves for garnish (optional)

Preheat oven to 400°F. Mix milk and cayenne. Pound chicken between layer of wax paper until breasts flatten a bit. Marinate chicken in milk mixture for 10 minutes.

Mix salt and pepper into cornmeal. Remove chicken from milk and roll in cornmeal, making sure to completely coat chicken. Dip chicken into egg white and roll in pecans. In a large skillet, melt butter and add oil. When it is hot, brown chicken breasts quickly on both sides, about 2½ minutes total. Remove to a baking dish and place in oven 6–7 minutes to finish the cooking. Serve immediately, garnished with pink grapefruit sections and basil or mint leaves, if desired.

LIME-BAKED CHICKEN PIECES

This snappy chicken dish calls for assertive side dishes. Serve with Mia-Mex Star Fruit and Black Bean Salsa (page 27) or Black Bean Soup (page 78) or on a bed of Easy Black Bean Purée (page 31). Add some steamed white rice and Pink Coleslaw (page 68), and garnish with fresh-snipped chives.

Serves 4

- 4 fresh thyme sprigs
- 1 bay leaf
- ½ cup No-Cook Mojito (page 40)
- 2 tbsp Lime-Chive Butter Log (page 46), butter or margarine
- ½ cup all-purpose flour
- 1 tsp salt
- ½ tsp fresh-ground black pepper
- fresh-snipped chives to garnish (optional)

Stir thyme and bay leaf into Mojito. Marinate chicken in this mixture 2 hours or overnight.

Preheat oven to 350°F and butter a roasting pan. Drain marinade and discard. Melt remaining Lime-Chive Butter, butter or margarine. Combine flour, salt and pepper. Dredge chicken pieces in the flour mixture and shake off excess. Put chicken pieces in oven, drizzle with the melted butter and bake until well browned, 50–55 minutes.

RIGHT
LIME-BAKED CHICKEN PIECES

BROILED OR GRILLED LIME CHICKEN BREASTS

Sweet peppers lend extra pizazz to this simple dish. Throw some red and yellow peppers on the grill while you're at it, or serve with Sweet Pepper Chutney (page 43), Lime-Pepper Noodles (page 110) and Chayote and Carrots (page 114).

Serves 4

- 4 skinned boneless chicken breasts, trimmed of fat, halved and tendon cut to flatten
- ⅓ cup olive oil
- fresh-squeezed juice of 3 limes
- 4 cloves garlic, minced
- 3 tbsp chopped fresh cilantro
- ½ tsp *each* salt and fresh-ground black pepper

Pound chicken between layer of wax paper to flatten more. In a bowl, combine olive oil, lime juice, garlic, 2 tbsp cilantro, salt and pepper. Pour over chicken and marinate at least 1 hour.

Grill or broil the chicken breasts 2 minutes on each side. Remove to platter. Sprinkle with remaining cilantro and serve immediately.

STOVETOP CREAMY CHICKEN

This one has a rich, creamy taste but need not wreck your diet if you use reduced-fat sour cream rather than the heavy-duty stuff. I like to pair it with Mango Soup (page 77), Plantain-Apple Patties (page 114) and Passion Fruit Cup (page 70).

Serves 4

- 2 tbsp vegetable oil
- 2 tbsp Lime-Chive Butter (page 44), butter or margarine
- 4 skinned boneless chicken breasts, trimmed of fat
- 1½ cups canned chicken broth
- 1 tsp crumbled thyme leaves
- 1 cup sour cream, or reduced-fat sour cream
- ½ tsp cornstarch
- ½ cup No Cook Mojito (page 40)

In large skillet over medium heat, heat oil and butter. Add chicken breasts and sauté until golden, about 2 minutes on each side. Add broth and thyme and bring to a boil. Lower heat, cover and simmer 15 minutes or until chicken is cooked through and juices run clear. Remove chicken to warm platter. In small bowl, stir together sour cream and cornstarch. Stir in Mojito until blended. Stir into juice in skillet. Simmer 2 minutes, stirring occasionally, until slightly thickened. Pour over chicken and serve immediately.

POACHED CHICKEN WITH MELON

This unusual and refreshing chilled dish looks 5-star restaurant pretty when served with wild rice or Gingery Jasmine Rice (page 118). Instead of a tossed salad, try chilled asparagus drizzled with Curry-Lime Vinaigrette (page 39).

You might want to serve this on chilled plates. Glass or crystal plates are perfect.

Serves 4

- 1½ cups canned low-sodium chicken broth
- 4 skinned, boneless chicken breasts, trimmed of fat
- 3 tbsp red wine vinegar
- 1 tbsp firmly packed dark brown sugar
- 2 cloves garlic, minced
- 1 tsp minced fresh ginger root
- 1 tsp Dijon mustard
- ½ cup diced mango
- ¼ cup honeydew melon balls
- ¼ cup cantaloupe balls
- fresh-snipped chives to garnish (optional)

In a medium skillet, bring broth to a boil, then reduce heat to low and simmer. Add chicken, cover and simmer, until cooked through and the juices run clear, 8–10 minutes. With slotted spatula, remove chicken from skillet. Leave to cool, then cover and refrigerate until chilled, 2 hours.

Meanwhile, boil broth until reduced to ¼ cup. Stir in remaining ingredients, except melon balls, and cook, stirring frequently, 5 minutes. Gently stir in melon balls and diced mango. Toss to coat. Refrigerate until chilled, 2 hours. Garnish with snipped chives and serve.

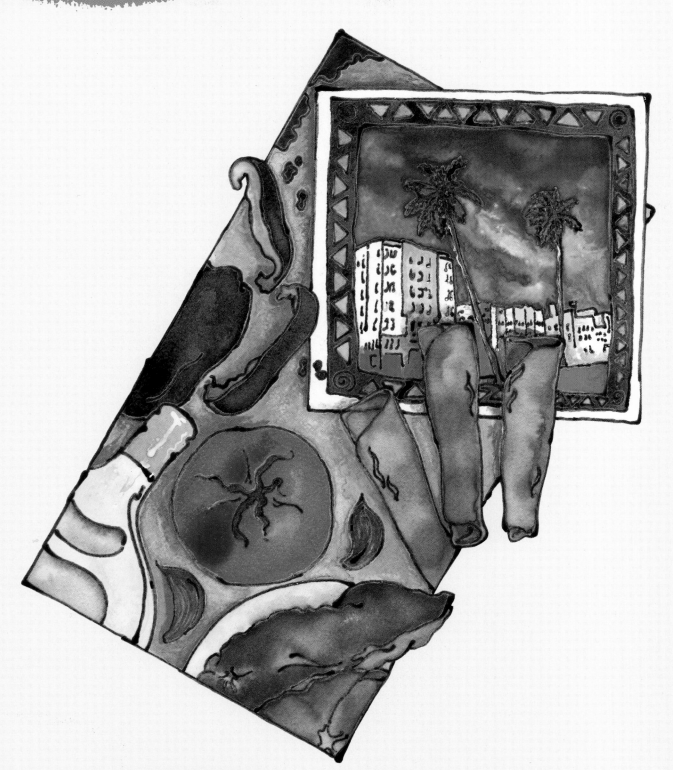

Meat Dishes

BOLICHE (CUBAN POT ROAST)

If there's such a thing as a gourmet pot roast, this is it. I have fiddled with many different recipes for it, but this one – with a few Nuevo Cuban innovations, notably the sesame coating – works well in sealing in the juices. Serve with garlicky mashed potatoes, lima beans in Warm Citrus-Mushroom Salsa (page 30) and, if you have any room left after this filling meal, Catalan Creme Brulée (page 121).

Serves 4–6

- 3-lb eye of round roast
- 1 cup plus 2 tbsp No-Cook Mojito (page 40)
- 2 tbsp sesame oil divided in half
- 4–6 oz chorizo sausage, casing removed and chopped
- ¼ cup finely diced smoked ham
- ⅛ cup chopped stuffed green olives
- 3 cloves garlic, minced
- ½ Spanish onion, chopped
- ¼ green bell pepper, seeded and chopped
- ¼ sweet red pepper, seeded and chopped
- ¼ cup sesame seeds
- 1½ tbsp dry bread crumbs
- 1 tsp salt
- 4 oz canned crushed tomatoes
- 1 bay leaf
- 4 potatoes, rinsed and quartered
- salt and fresh-ground black pepper to taste

If the roast you buy has a natural "eye," simply expand it with a sharp knife for a stuffing cavity. Otherwise, cut your own lengthwise pocket in the center of the meat. Pour 1 cup Mojito over meat, cover and refrigerate overnight, turning several times.

Remove roast from Mojito marinade and pat dry with paper towels. In a Dutch oven over a moderate heat, heat 1 tbsp sesame oil and brown meat on all sides. Remove to a platter and allow to cool.

In a bowl, mix together chorizo, ham, green olives, garlic, onion and peppers for stuffing. When roast is cool enough to touch, rub with 1 tbsp sesame oil and roll in mixture of sesame seeds, bread crumbs and 1 tsp salt. Stuff roast with stuffing mixture. Skewer the open end closed.

Meanwhile, preheat oven to 325°F, return meat to Dutch oven, cover and bake about 2 hours. After about 30 minutes, add crushed tomatoes, Mojito and bay leaf to bottom of Dutch oven. Cover and continue baking until the meat is fork tender, basting occasionally with the sauce at the bottom of the pot. (If you'd like to serve potatoes with your boliche, add them about 40 minutes before cooking time is complete.)

Remove bay leaf. Remove roast (and potatoes, if you have added them) from pan, season crushed tomatoes and natural juices in the pan with salt and pepper and transfer to a gravy boat for serving over the meat when carved.

RIGHT A vivid red bougainvillea against an old fashioned white picket fence.

GRILLED ISLA BONITA PORK

Island spices give this pizazz. Try it with Pineapple Salsa (page 29), White Bean & Yuca Vichyssoise (page 72) or Pink Coleslaw (page 68) for a taste of the tropics even on a snowy day.

Serves 4

- ½ tbsp ground ginger
- ½ tbsp ground cinnamon
- ½ tbsp grated nutmeg
- ½ tsp dry mustard
- 4 pork tenderloins, 4–6 oz each, trimmed of fat
- vegetable oil or cooking spray for grilling
- pineapple wedges (optional)

In a small bowl, combine ginger, cinnamon, nutmeg and dry mustard, and stir well. Pat pork dry with paper towel. Rub pork with spice mixture. Place in a shallow dish, cover and chill 30 minutes.

Coat grill rack with cooking spray and place tenderloins on grill rack over medium coals (page 86) about 5 inches from heat. Cover and cook, turning occasionally, until meat thermometer registers 160°F, about 25 minutes. Cut into ½-inch thick slices. Garnish with pineapple, if desired.

ROPA VIEJA

In Spanish, the literal translation is "old clothes" because, frankly, that's how drab a pile of shredded beef looks. This dish looks smashing, though, helped immensely by some extra Sofrito (page 38). I like to present *Rope* "Nuevo-style," tucked inside warmed flour tortillas, with a bowl of Sofrito on the table for spooning extra spiciness atop. *Ropa* is also good served over Herbed Rice Cakes (page 108).

Serves 4–6

- 2 lb skirt or flank steak
- 1 large onion, halved
- 1 large onion, thinly sliced
- 4 cloves garlic, finely chopped
- 1 large celery rib, chopped
- 1 tbsp salt
- ¼ cup olive oil
- 1 large green bell pepper, seeded and cut into thin lengthwise strips
- 3 large ripe tomatoes, about 1½ lb, finely diced
- ½ cup dry white wine, or 2 tbsp dry sherry
- 2 bay leaves
- 2 tbsp ground cumin
- ¼ cup cooked sweet peas at room temperature (optional)
- salt and fresh-ground black pepper to taste
- ⅓ cup canned pimientos, drained and chopped for garnish (optional)

Place the skirt steak in a large stockpot and add water to cover completely. Add halved onion, the halved garlic, celery and salt and bring to a boil. Cover, reduce heat to moderate and cook until meat is tender, about 1¼ hours. Transfer meat to a plate, leave to cool, cover and refrigerate until chilled.

Shred chilled meat with your fingers and set aside. If it doesn't shred easily, pound it between a layer of wax paper and it should easily pull apart.

In a large skillet, heat olive oil. Add remaining, finely chopped garlic and cook over high heat until lightly browned, about 1 minute. Reduce heat to moderate and stir in sliced onion and bell pepper. Cook, stirring occasionally, until softened, about 10 minutes.

Stir in tomatoes, wine or sherry, bay leaves, cumin and a pinch of salt. Increase the heat to moderately high and cook, stirring occasionally, about 25 minutes. Remove bay leaves. Add shredded meat, stir, and cook about 5 minutes, until meat is heated. Stir in peas, if desired, and remove from heat. Season with salt and pepper. Garnish, if desired, and serve immediately.

POP-EYE'S PORK TENDERLOIN

Place a scoop of Pineapple Salsa (page 29), Pineapple-Coconut Relish (page 31) or Tomato-Ginger Chutney (page 42) next to this pretty dish, add some Plantain-Apple Patties (page 114) and Pasta with Beans (page 116) and get ready for oohs and aahs.

Serves 4

- 4 tsp olive oil, divided
- 1 large clove garlic
- ¾ lb spinach, rinsed and stems removed
- 4 tsp all-purpose flour
- ¾ tsp salt
- ¼ tsp fresh-ground black pepper
- ¼ tsp paprika
- ⅛ tsp cayenne pepper
- 4 pork tenderloins, 4–6 oz each, trimmed of fat and sliced ½-inch thick

In a skillet over medium heat, heat 2 tsp oil. Add garlic and cook, stirring, until barely browned, about 1 minute. Remove from skillet. Add spinach leaves and cook, stirring, until wilted. Keep warm on serving platter.

Combine flour, salt, pepper, paprika and cayenne in plastic or heavy paper bag. Pat pork dry with paper towels. Add pork slices to bag and shake to coat.

In skillet over high heat, heat remaining 2 tsp oil. Add pork and sauté, turning occasionally, just until cooked through, 4–5 minutes. Arrange pork on spinach and serve immediately.

ELEGANTE PICADILLO

This was popular served on hamburger buns in the 1950s as a dish called Sloppy Joes. My mother used to make it for my high school girlfriends when they came to our house for slumber parties. I always thought they were called Sloppy Joes because they were messy. Later, I learned that picadillo was served in both a Havana and a Key West bar called Sloppy Joe's. Ernest Hemingway is said to have frequented the one in Cuba when he lived there and definitely frequented its counterpart in Key West, where he also made his home at one time.

This version is a far cry from either the Sloppy Joes of my youth or the bar food Hemingway might have enjoyed, although I don't think he would have objected at all to the addition of liqueur. This complex dish is served here in onion "bowls." Begin your meal with Black Bean Soup (page 78), then serve the Picadillo over Herbed Rice Cakes (page 108) and top off the meal with Mango Sorbet (page 126).

Use a small knife to cut off ½ inch of each onion's stem end in a sawtooth pattern. Remove and reserve the inner portion of each onion (a melon baller works well, leaving the outer 2 layers intact). Mince the reserved onions (about 2 cups) for the stuffing.

Preheat oven to 350°F. In a large skillet, heat 2 tsp oil. Sauté onion until softened, about 10 minutes. Add garlic, sauté about 30 seconds. Add ground beef and sauté until browned, about 5 minutes. Reduce heat, add Grand Marnier and carefully ignite. When flames subside, add remaining ingredients, including ¾ tsp salt and ¼ tsp pepper. Cook over low heat, stirring occasionally to blend flavors, about 10 minutes.

Brush the cavity and outer surface of each onion with remaining oil. Spoon a portion of the stuffing mixture into each onion. Transfer stuffed onions to a small baking pan. Bake until onions are tender and golden brown, about 40 minutes. Serve immediately.

Serves 4

- 4 large onions, peeled
- 2 tbsp olive oil
- 2 large cloves garlic, minced
- 1¼ lb lean ground beef
- ½ cup Grand Marnier liqueur
- ½ cup dark raisins
- ⅓ cup pimento-stuffed olives, thinly sliced crosswise
- 2 tbsp capers, drained
- ⅓ cup tomato paste
- ½ tsp ground cumin
- ¼ tsp dried oregano
- salt and fresh-ground black pepper to taste

RIGHT A typical street scene in Key West, Florida.

PURPLE PEPPERED PENNE WITH CHORIZO

Sounds like a dish Peter Pepper would like. Actually, anyone would. It's a lovely one-dish meal that combines the Cubans' long-time love of Spanish chorizo with their relatively new love of pasta. Serve with Chayote and Carrots (page 114) or Sauteéd Chayote and Corn (page 110) and Passion Fruit Cup (page 70).

Serves 4

- 2 eggplants, halved crosswise and cut into ¼-inch thick slices
- 7 tbsp olive oil
- salt and fresh-ground black pepper to taste
- 1 lb chorizo or good smoked sausage, casing removed and cut into ¼-inch thick slices
- one 4-oz jar roasted sweet red peppers, drained and coarsely chopped, or 1 roasted
- sweet red pepper, peeled, seeded and coarsely chopped
- 1 clove garlic, minced
- 1 tomato, peeled, seeded and finely diced
- ½ cup minced fresh cilantro
- 1 tsp balsamic vinegar
- 2 tbsp fresh-squeezed lime juice
- 12 oz penne, macaroni, or pasta shells

Preheat oven to 350°F. Brush eggplant slices with 3 tbsp oil, then sprinkle salt and pepper. Place eggplant and chorizo in a baking pan and cover with foil. Bake until eggplant is tender, about 20 minutes. Remove eggplant slices, cut them into small dice and set aside.

Mix sausage and eggplant with red peppers, garlic, tomato, cilantro, vinegar and lime juice. Season with ½ tsp salt and ¼ tsp pepper or to taste and set aside.

Meanwhile, in a soup kettle, bring 6 quarts of water to a boil. Add 1 tbsp salt and penne. Cook *al dente*, about 10 minutes. Drain penne and transfer to a large serving bowl. Add remaining oil and chorizo mixture. Toss to combine and serve immediately.

Side Dishes

CORN CUBANA

The beauty of this dish is that it's so easy to prepare, yet looks company-worthy. Serve it with just about any entrée, or try serving it with one of the appetizers in this book and you've got a meal!

Serves 4

- ½ lb chorizo, cooked, casing removed, and finely chopped, or bacon, cooked and crumbled
- 1 large onion, chopped
- two 15-oz cans whole kernel sweet corn, drained of all but 1 tbsp juices
- one 8-oz can tomato sauce
- fresh-ground black pepper

In a large skillet, fry chorizo and onion together until onions are tender. Set aside to cool. Add 1 tbsp corn juice and tomato sauce to chorizo drippings and cook slowly, stirring frequently, about 1 hour. Season with the pepper to taste. Add corn and cook 1 minute. Before serving, spread chorizo over the top of the corn-tomato mixture.

HERBED RICE CAKES

A variation on an old favorite, rice croquettes, these herbed cakes were popularized in Miami by Yuca, the Nuevo Cubano restaurant. Garnish with a dollop of sour cream sprinkled with some of the chives. These are great with thick Black Bean Soup (page 78), Ropa Vieja (page 102) and as an alternate to potatoes with almost any entrée.

Serves 4–6

- 2 cups cooked rice
- 1 egg, lightly beaten
- 1 small onion, minced
- 2 tbsp finely chopped fresh parsley
- 1 tomato, finely chopped
- 1 bunch chives, finely chopped
- 1 bunch thyme, finely chopped
- 1–2 tbsp olive oil for frying
- 4 tbsp sour cream for garnish (optional)

Combine rice, egg, onion 1⅓ tbsp parsley, tomato, chives and thyme. Pat into 6 large or 12 small patties.

In a heavy-bottomed skillet over medium-high heat, fry rice cakes, turning once, until golden brown, on both sides. Cook in batches if necessary. Drain on paper towels, garnish, if desired, and serve immediately.

SO-SWEET SWEET POTATOES & CARROTS

This dish offers a variety of tastes and textures, and couldn't be more colorful. For a very special occasion, garnish with the orange slices, pecans and toasted coconut as instructed below.

Serves 4

- ¾ lb carrots, sliced into ½-inch thick rounds (about 2 cups)
- ¾ lb sweet potatoes, peeled and cubed (about 2 cups)
- one 16-oz can unsweetened pineapple chunks, undrained
- ¼ cup water
- 2 tbsp brown sugar
- 1 tbsp cornstarch, dissolved in 1 tbsp cold water
- 2 tsp soy sauce
- 1 tsp vinegar
- ½ tsp grated orange zest
- ⅛ tsp salt
- ¼ cup golden raisins
- 2 seedless navel oranges, peeled and thinly sliced (optional)
- 2 oz pecan halves for garnish (optional)
- 2 tsp shredded coconut for garnish (optional)

In a vegetable steamer over boiling water, steam carrots 2 minutes. Add sweet potatoes, cover and steam until tender but not mushy, 8–10 minutes. Set aside.

Drain pineapple, reserving ½ cup juice. Combine juice, water, sugar, cornstarch, soy, vinegar, zest and salt in a saucepan. Place over medium heat and bring to a boil, stirring. Add pineapple and raisins and simmer 1 minute. Combine vegetables and pineapple mixture in a large bowl and stir gently. Serve now or proceed to next step, if garnish is desired.

Preheat oven to 350°F. Line sides of an 8-inch ovenproof serving dish with overlapping oranges. Scoop contents of bowl into dish and sprinkle top with pecans and coconut. Place in oven for 10 minutes or until coconut browns lightly.

SAUTEÉD CHAYOTE AND CORN

Here's an alternative to the steamed combination. The chayote adds a flavor to the corn that does not overwhelm it as, say, green peppers would, yet chayote has a similar snappy texture.

Serves 4

- 2 chayotes, peeled, pitted and cut into 1-inch cubes
- fresh-cut kernels from 3 ears yellow corn, or 2 cups frozen corn, thawed
- ½ tbsp any butter log (page 44–51), butter or margarine
- salt and fresh-ground black pepper to taste

Bring a pot of water to a boil and add chayote. When water returns to a boil, drain chayote and rinse for a couple of minutes under cold running water. In a large skillet, heat ½ tsp butter log, butter or margarine and sauté the chayote cubes until tender, about 4 minutes. Add corn and continue to sauté 3–4 more minutes. Season with salt and pepper.

BELOW The brilliant colors of the fruit are almost overshadowed by the color of the market stall itself.

RIGHT
LIME-PEPPER NOODLES

YUCA FRIES

Serve with Simple Garlicky Aioli (page 32), Tomato-Ginger Chutney (page 42) or Pepper-Lime Dip (page 33).

Serves 4

- 8 garlic cloves
- 2 bay leaves
- 2½ tbsp salt
- 3 quarts water
- 1¼–1½ lb yuca, scrubbed, peeled and halved lengthwise, or substitute potatoes
- vegetable oil for frying

In a saucepan, combine garlic, bay leaves, 2 tbsp salt and water and bring to a boil. Add yuca or potatoes and simmer until tender but not mushy or sticky, 30–40 minutes.

Drain, pat dry with paper towels and, when cool enough to handle, cut into French fries. In a large skillet, heat ½-inch of oil to 375°F. Sprinkle yuca fries with remaining salt and fry until golden. Drain fries on paper towels and serve piping hot.

LIME-PEPPER NOODLES

It's difficult to believe that a dish this simple could taste so good. I like to add bits of leftover pork or chicken and vegetables to make a one-dish meal.

Serves 4

- one 12-oz package egg noodles
- 2 tbsp Island Citrus Butter Log (page 50), melted
- salt and fresh-ground black pepper to taste
- 1 lime, decoratively sliced for garnish (optional)

Cook noodles in boiling salted water until *al dente*. Drain. Toss noodles in Citrus Butter, then season with salt and pepper. Garnish with limes and serve immediately.

PLANTAIN ROUNDS WITH BRIE

Also known as Tostones con Brie. *Tostone* is Cuban slang for "twice-fried green plantain." If you prefer a plainer side dish or snack, simply skip the Brie and eat these dipped in Ginger-Orange Mayo (page 32), or doused with No-Cook Mojito (page 40).

Serves 4

- 3 green, unripe plantains, peeled and cut into ½-inch thick rounds
- 4 tbsp vegetable oil
- 2 tsp garlic powder
- ¼ lb ripe Brie, rinds removed

In a large skillet, heat oil to 350°F. Fry about 10 pieces of plantain at a time for about 2 minutes. Drain on paper towels and allow *tostones* to cool enough to handle. Repeat until all the pieces of plantain are fried, keeping the oil hot.

Press each *tostone* between 2 wooden cheese boards by putting weight on the top board – or, if you have a sandwich maker or waffle iron, press *tostones* in one of those.

Reheat oil to 375°F, sprinkle oil evenly with garlic powder and fry *tostones* again until golden. Drain on paper towels. Spread 1–2 tsp Brie atop each *tostone*. Place *tostone* on a cookie sheet and pop under broiler for a few seconds to warm Brie, then serve.

OVEN-BAKED TROPICAL CHIPS TWO-WAYS

Here's a low-fat, low-calorie chip recipe. I like to douse these with No-Cook Mojito (page 40) or dip them in one of the mayos, salsas or chutneys in the first chapter.

Serves 4

- 2 egg whites
- 1½ tbsp chili powder (for spicy-hot), or allspice (for spicy-sweet)
- 4 boniatos, peeled and sliced into thin chips
- vegetable cooking spray
- salt and fresh-ground black pepper to taste

Preheat oven to 450°F. In a large bowl, lightly beat egg whites with a fork until foamy. Stir in either chili powder or allspice. Add boniatos and toss to coat well. Spread chips in a single layer on a cookie sheet sprayed with vegetable oil. Bake until potatoes are crisp and browned, 30–35 minutes. Season with salt and pepper.

CHAYOTE AND CARROTS

The ten or so fanciful names chayote goes by in various parts of the world would take more space to list than this recipe does. Suffice it to say the word "chayote" comes from the Aztec language, and the pale-green, squashlike member of the gourd family has been eaten for centuries. Some say it tastes like a combination of apples, cucumbers, zucchini and kohlrabi. Since it must be cooked, it's important that its crisp texture holds up. Some of the highest quality, most durable chayote is being exported by Costa Rica. Toss with a sweet or herbal butter, depending on your main dish and your mood.

Serves 4

- ½ cup water
- 1 tsp sugar
- ½ tsp chicken consommé granules
- 3 chayotes, peeled, pitted and cut into 1-inch chunks
- 3 carrots, peeled and cut into ½-inch thick slices
- 2 tbsp any butter log (pages 44–51), butter or margarine
- salt and fresh-ground black pepper to taste
- 1 tbsp chopped fresh parsley for garnish (optional)

In a large saucepan, combine water, sugar and consommé granules. Add the carrots and bring to a boil, then reduce heat and simmer until tender, about 25 minutes. About five minutes before the carrots are cooked, add the chayotes and continue simmering until both are cooked.

In a large skillet, melt 2 tbsp butter log of your choice or butter. Add drained vegetables. Stir to coat with butter and season with salt and pepper to taste. Garnish, if desired, and serve.

PLANTAIN-APPLE PATTIES

Apples, which can't be grown in the tropics, are not traditional to Cuban cuisine, but they are sought after delicacies, especially on holidays. Combining "exotic" apples with plantains, this inspired dish can be festooned with crumbled bacon, and complements ham and pork dishes.

Thoroughly mix together grated plantains and apples. Add onion, cinnamon, garlic, egg white, salt and pepper. In a skillet, heat butter and oil. Spoon large tablespoonfuls of the mixture into skillet and sauté until golden. Turn and brown the other side. Drain on paper towels before serving.

Serves 4

- 2 ripe black plantains, peeled and grated
- 2 tart cooking apples, pared, cored and grated
- ½ cup chopped onion
- 2 tsp ground cinnamon
- 2 large cloves garlic, crushed
- 1 egg white
- salt and fresh-ground black pepper to taste
- 1 tbsp butter or margarine
- 1 tbsp oil
- 1 slice bacon, fried, drained and crumbled for garnish (optional)

RIGHT
PLANTAIN-APPLE PATTIES

PASTA WITH BEANS, CUBAN STYLE

This can stand alone if you stir in some leftover cubed pork, ham, or sausage, but I adore it as a side dish with fish entrées, especially Crisp Oven-Fried Flounder (page 88). This is so colorful with its yellow, red, green and black hues.

Serves 4

- 1 lb dried tri-color fusili pasta (twists)
- 3 tbsp olive oil
- ½ tbsp chili powder
- 2 tbsp finely chopped garlic
- 3 tbsp drained and finely chopped sun-dried tomatoes packed in oil
- 3 tbsp finely chopped scallions
- 2 tbsp finely chopped fresh ginger root
- grated zest or 1 orange
- 2 tbsp coarsely chopped cooked black beans
- 2 tsp sugar
- 3 tbsp tomato paste
- 1 cup drained and coarsely chopped canned tomatoes
- ½ cup chicken stock
- salt and fresh-ground black pepper to taste
- extra scallions for garnish (optional)

Bring a large pot of salted water to a rolling boil and cook the pasta *al dente*. Drain and set aside.

In a large skillet, heat olive oil, then add chili powder, garlic, tomatoes, scallions, ginger, orange zest and beans. Stir-fry this mixture 1 minute. Add cooked pasta and stir-fry another minute. Add sugar, tomato paste, chopped tomatoes, chicken stock and salt and pepper. Stir-fry 2 more minutes, until pasta is thoroughly coated with the seasonings. Serve immediately.

CURRIED ALMOND RICE

Cubans adore peas, especially small sweet ones which they call by the French name *petit-pois.* Cubans love rice even more. Many homemakers buy it in 20-pound sacks. But whereas tradition favors plain white rice, Nuevo cuisine is more adventurous, as you will see in this mouth-watering dish.

Serves 4

- 1 tbsp Curry Butter Log (page 44), butter or margarine, softened
- 3 cups water
- 1½ cups converted rice
- ½ cup frozen green peas, thawed and cooked (optional)
- 2 tbsp sliced almonds, toasted, if desired

In an 8-inch skillet, melt Curry Butter, butter or margarine. Stir in water. Cover and heat to boiling. Stir in rice, reduce heat, cover and simmer about 15 minutes. Add peas at end just long enough to heat. Sprinkle with almonds and serve.

GINGERY JASMINE RICE

Use the finest rice you can find for this dish, and the result will be a creamy risotto-like texture. I like to add bits of leftover meat, fish or seafood to this for a one-dish meal.

Serves 4

- 1½ cup jasmine, basmati or Texmati rice
- ¼ tsp ground cumin
- 1 tsp Smoked Pineapple Butter Log (page 46), butter or margarine
- 1 cup water
- 1 tsp grated fresh ginger root

Rinse rice in cold water several times until water runs clear, then drain. In a medium saucepan, sauté cumin in butter log, butter or margarine about 30 seconds. Stir in rice, water and ginger. Bring to a boil, then cover, reduce heat to very low and cook 12 minutes without lifting the lid.

Remove pan from the heat and let sit, covered, at least 5 and up to 20 minutes. Before serving, fluff rice with a fork.

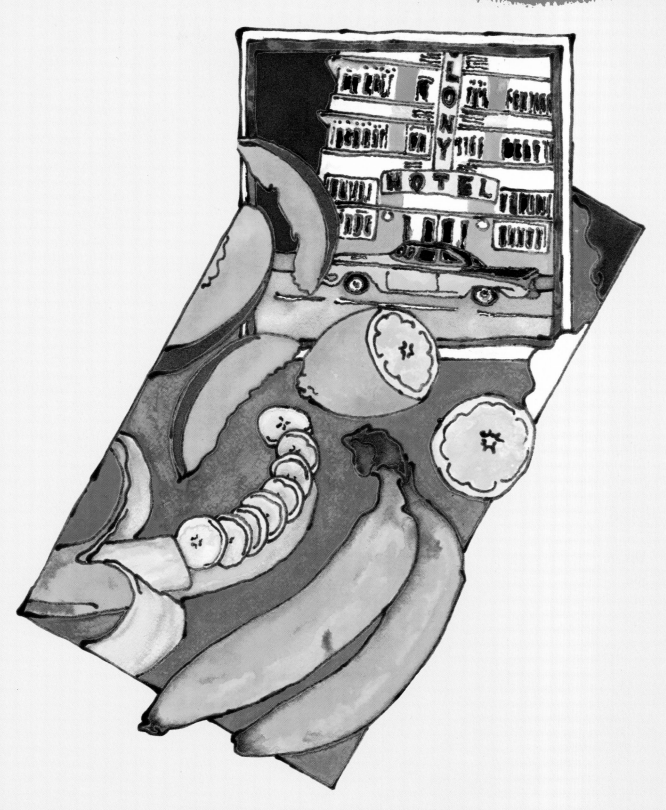

Desserts

No-Cook Rum Chiquitas

I would say making this dish is as easy as pie, but that would be incorrect. It's easier than pie.

Serves 4

- 2–4 ripe bananas, sliced crosswise
- ¼ cup rum
- 2 tbsp sugar
- 2 tsp cinnamon
- ¼ tsp grated nutmeg
- fresh orange slices for garnish
- banana leaves, cut into strips for serving

Place the bananas in a bowl. Pour rum over them and sprinkle with the sugar and spices. Allow to marinate about 1 hour.

Arrange strips of banana leaves in bottom of glass serving bowl just before serving for additional color, then pile the banana slices on top and garnish with slices of fresh orange.

BELOW A mobile market – fresh fruit being sold from the back of a truck.

CATALAN CREME BRULÉE

French-style custard desserts have held sway in Miami restaurants ever since the Cuban community ventured beyond flan, the Spanish caramel custard. This is one of the featured desserts at Mark's Place, one of Miami's landmark Nuevo restaurants. While Miami is awash in Key limes, lemons are used in this dish to make it less tart and more delicate.

Serves 6

- ¾ cup sugar
- 7 egg yolks
- ¾ quart heavy cream
- peel of 1 orange cut into thin slices
- peel of 1 lemon cut into thin slices
- 1 cinnamon stick
- ¾ tsp bitter almond extract, or regular almond extract
- 6 tbsp light brown sugar

Whisk together sugar and egg yolks and set aside. In a heavy saucepan stir heavy cream, orange and lemon peels, cinnamon stick and almond extract together and bring to a boil. Remove the peels and cinnamon stick. Pour flavored cream mixture into the egg yolks very slowly, stirring constantly.

Meanwhile, preheat oven to 350°F. Pour into 6 individual ramekins or custard cups. Place ramekins in a baking pan and add enough water to come about half way up the sides. Bake about 30 minutes, or until custard has set. Let cool in refrigerator.

Just before serving, sprinkle each ramekin evenly with about 1 tbsp light brown sugar. Place ramekins under broiler for a few seconds, until sugar burns. Set aside for 10–15 minutes and serve.

WHITE CHOCOLATE COCONUT TART

Move over dark chocolate. In Miami, folks fancy their chocolate white and bright, like our sunshine and our frothy surf. And this combination of coconut and white chocolate is as smooth as a ballad by Miami's own Gloria Estefan.

Serves 8

- 1 sheet refrigerated piecrust, thawed if frozen
- 2 tsp cornstarch
- 2 tbsp sugar
- 4 egg yolks
- 2 tbsp dark rum
- ¼ cup plus 2 tbsp water
- ¼ cup (½ stick) unsalted butter, softened
- 8 oz white chocolate candy bar, chopped
- ¾ cup shredded unsweetened coconut
- ¾ cup heavy cream, whipped
- ⅓ cup shredded sweetened coconut, toasted, for garnish
- white chocolate curls, for garnish (optional), pared from a white chocolate bar

Preheat oven to 400°F. Follow package directions for unfolding crust into 9- × 1-inch round tart pan with removable bottom. Fold excess crust into pan. Press firmly against sides, making crust even with top of pan. Prick bottom and sides with fork. Line shell with aluminum foil and fill with dry beans or rice. Place on cookie sheet. Bake on bottom oven rack for 15 minutes. Remove foil and beans. Bake until browned and fully baked, about 12 more minutes. Remove from oven and place on wire rack to cool completely.

In top of double boiler, combine cornstarch and sugar. Whisk in yolks until smooth. Stir in rum and ¼ cup water. Cook over simmering water, whisking constantly and vigorously until very thick and smooth, about 15–20 minutes. Do not boil. Remove from water. Stir in butter until combined. Pour into medium-size bowl. Leave to cool, then cover and refrigerate.

Clean top of double boiler. In top of double boiler over simmering water, melt together the remaining 2 tbsp water and chocolate, stirring occasionally, until smooth. Remove from water. Whisk into rum mixture. Let cool, then cover and refrigerate until cold, about 45 minutes.

Fold coconut and whipped cream into rum mixture. Pour into tart shell. Refrigerate at least 2 hours.

KEY LIME PIE

This pie will never go out of style.

Serves 4

- 4 egg yolks
- one 15-oz can sweetened condensed milk
- ½ cup fresh-squeezed lime juice from Key, Persian or regular limes
- 9-inch baked pie sheet or graham cracker piecrust, thawed if frozen
- extra whipped cream for serving

Whip egg yolks and blend with condensed milk. Add lime juice, mixing only until juice is mixed in. Do not overbeat. Pour into baked pie shell or piecrust. Chill until set (overnight is best). Top with whipped cream if you like.

CHURROS

Cuban-Americans sell these licorice-flavored Spanish doughnuts at intersections in Miami. Try this easy-to-make, version for dessert, Sunday breakfast or for a snack.

Serves 4

- 3 tbsp sugar for dusting
- 1 tsp ground anise seed or cinnamon if you prefer
- vegetable oil for frying
- one 10-oz canister of refrigerated, ready-to-bake biscuits

Place sugar and anise or cinnamon in a heavy brown paper grocery bag, close bag with your fist and shake to mix.

In a large kettle, large saucepan or large skillet, heat 2 inches vegetable oil to 400°F, or heat oil in electric deep fat fryer following manufacturing directions. A drop of batter will sizzle when it hits the oil.

Pull each biscuit apart in quarters and drop from long-handled tongs into oil. Turn with tongs or a slotted spoon until golden. Drain on paper towels, toss in bag with sugar and anise, shake to dust, and serve immediately.

CAFÉ CON LECHE CUSTARD

This dessert, which is a favorite at Key West's Palm Grill, combines the love Cuban-Americans have for *café con leche* – espresso coffee laced with steaming milk and sugar – with their love of custard.

Serves 4

- 4 tbsp cornstarch
- 3 cups milk
- 1 cup heavy cream
- 2½ tbsp instant coffee powder
- 1 cup sugar
- 2 eggs
- whipped cream, chocolate-covered espresso beans for garnish

Stir cornstarch into 1 cup of milk, stirring until smooth. In top of double boiler, place all the remaining ingredients, except the eggs and garnish, and stir in cornstarch mixture. Stir over medium-high heat until thickened. Cover and simmer 10 minutes.

Beat eggs well. Slowly add 1 cup of hot coffee mixture to the eggs, beating continually. Pour egg mixture into remaining coffee mixture in the double boiler, still over heat, and beat well to incorporate. Cover and simmer 2 minutes. Remove from heat and pour into coffee cups. Cover with plastic wrap, leave to cool and then refrigerate. When chilled, top with fresh whipped cream and 1 chocolate-covered espresso bean.

RIGHT
CAFÉ CON LECHE CUSTARD

SENSUOUS SORBETS

The word sorbet comes from the Arab *charab*, meaning refreshing drink. The ancients would be mystified by some modern New American renditions of "ices," sorbets featuring poblano chiles and cactus pears and persimmons. In Miami, chefs and cooks aren't tempted to such extremes. Instead, they are having fun making sorbets from Florida's largesse of tropical fruits.

Serves 4

- 2 mamey sapotes, mangos or cantaloupes, peeled, seeded and cut into large chunks
- 1 envelope unflavored gelatin
- ½ cup water
- ½ cup light corn syrup
- ½ cup lemon juice
- ¼ tsp salt
- fresh mint sprigs for garnish

In blender set at medium speed or in food processor with a knife blade attached, blend melon chunks until smooth. Pour into 9- by 9-inch metal baking pan.

In a 1-quart saucepan, evenly sprinkle gelatin over water and let stand 1 minute to soften. Stir over medium heat until gelatin completely dissolves. Whisk gelatin mixture, corn syrup, lemon juice and salt into puréed melon. Cover baking pan tightly with heavy-duty aluminum foil. Freeze until partially frozen, stirring occasionally to prevent ice crystals from forming, about 3 hours.

Spoon sorbet mixture into chilled food processor bowl with knife blade attached and blend until fluffy but do not allow to melt. (Or, spoon into chilled large bowl and beat with electric mixer at medium speed until fluffy.) Return mixture to baking pan, cover with heavy foil again and freeze until firm, about 2 hours.

Remove from freezer about 15 minutes before serving to soften a little. Scoop into parfait glasses or on dessert dishes. Garnish with mint sprigs.

GUAVA FOOL

Once upon a time, the word fool or *loca,* was not a pejorative, but was an affectionate term as "honey" is today, and this fruit-sugar-and-whipped-cream concoction was named after the term of endearment. Here's a nuevo, tropical version of the old-fashion dessert.

Serves 4

- 4 ripe guavas, trimmed and cut into 1-inch pieces
- 8–12 tsp confectioners' sugar
- ½ cup heavy cream

In a blender or food processor, purée guavas with half the sugar. Taste and add more sugar, if desired, and purée again. Repeat if necessary to add more sweetness.

Press mixture through a strainer, cover and chill. Before serving, whip cream and fold it into the purée in a swirling pattern.

RIGHT
GUAVA FOOL

126

INDEX